Pra

DEEP
KINDNESS

• • • • • • •

"This is a must-read for parents (and everyone, really) everywhere—especially in today's charged atmosphere. Houston breathes life into tough-to-tackle topics with stories, practical activities, and meaningful reflections. Parents can and must use this book to help the next generation understand what true Kindness really means."

—Michele Borba, EdD, educational psychologist and
bestselling author of *UnSelfie: Why Empathetic Kids
Succeed in Our All-About-Me World*
and *Thrivers: The Surprising Reasons Why Some Kids
Struggle and Others Shine*

"*Deep Kindness* is a book for everyone—even the skeptic. In a raw and real and relatable way, Houston Kraft takes you on a journey to challenge your notion of what Kindness means and exactly why Deep Kindness can heal and transform our world. You will smile, and most likely tear up. You will learn and be pushed outside of your comfort zone. And, most importantly, you will end up with a greater understanding of why Kindness actually matters."

—Jaclyn Lindsey, cofounder & CEO of Kindness.org

"Motivational speaker Kraft (*Deep Kindness*) explains a demanding version of Kindness in this vibrant work. He contrasts his version of selfless and courageous Kindness that will heal the world with what he calls 'confetti' kindness that requires little thought or commitment. He provides tools for overcoming incompetence, insecurity, and inconvenience, arguing that incompetence can be changed with empathy and vulnerability, insecurity can be addressed by tackling embarrassment and shame, and the burden of inconvenience (such as necessary daily tasks and routines) can be minimized by building Kind habits. His advice often notes the need for careful consideration rather than assuming what someone wants (for instance, the kid eating alone in the lunchroom may not want company, or your company) and cautions against the 'unintentional arrogance' that can accompany good deeds. Kraft's clear definition of necessary reorientations readers should consider (like forgiveness as 'separating the person from the behavior' or reframing busyness as a matter of priorities) makes his suggestions accessible. Kraft's insistent but doable nudges toward self-sacrificing Kindness will resonate with those who enjoy the work of Piero Ferrucci."

—*Publishers Weekly*

DEEP KINDNESS

A REVOLUTIONARY GUIDE FOR THE WAY WE THINK, TALK, AND ACT IN KINDNESS

HOUSTON KRAFT

SIMON ELEMENT

New York   London   Toronto   Sydney   New Delhi

SIMON
ELEMENT

An Imprint of Simon & Schuster, Inc.
1230 Avenue of the Americas
New York, NY 10020

First Simon Element Paperback edition April 2022

This publication contains the opinions and ideas of its author. It is intended to provide helpful and informative material on the subjects addressed in the publication. It is sold with the understanding that the author and publisher are not engaged in rendering medical, health, or any other kind of personal, professional services in the book. The reader should consult his or her medical, health, or other competent professional before adopting any of the suggestions in this book or drawing inferences from it.

The author and publisher specifically disclaim all responsibility for any liability, loss, or risk, personal or otherwise, that is incurred as a consequence, directly or indirectly, of the use and application of any of the contents of this book.

SIMON ELEMENT and colophon are trademarks of Simon & Schuster, Inc.

For information about special discounts for bulk purchases, please contact Simon & Schuster Special Sales at 1-866-506-1949 or business@simonandschuster.com.

The Simon & Schuster Speakers Bureau can bring authors to your live event. For more information or to book an event, contact the Simon & Schuster Speakers Bureau at 1-866-248-3049 or visit our website at www.simonspeakers.com.

Interior design by Jennifer Chung

Manufactured in the United States of America

5 7 9 10 8 6 4

Library of Congress Cataloging-in-Publication Data
Names: Kraft, Houston, author.
Title: Deep kindness : a revolutionary guide for the way we think, talk, and act in kindness / by Houston Kraft.
Description: New York : Tiller Press, 2020. | Includes bibliographical references. | Summary: "Spread meaningful kindness every day with these anecdotes and actions that can help bring change to our lives, our relationships, and the world" —Provided by publisher.
Identifiers: LCCN 2020021263 (print) | LCCN 2020021264 (ebook) | ISBN 9781982163105 (hardcover) | ISBN 9781982163112 (ebook)
Subjects: LCSH: Kindness.
Classification: LCC BJ1533.K5 K73 2020 (print) | LCC BJ1533.K5 (ebook) | DDC 177/.7—dc23

LC record available at https://lccn.loc.gov/2020021263
LC ebook record available at https://lccn.loc.gov/2020021264

ISBN 978-1-9821-6310-5
ISBN 978-1-9821-8331-8 (pbk)
ISBN 978-1-9821-6311-2 (ebook)

This book is dedicated to all people seeking
to create a Kinder world. We need you.

I've learned about Kindness from a lot of people.
My parents, Brad and Lesa, have been nothing but supportive
my entire life, and to have champions like that who
are forever in your corner is a gift that affects generations.

The influence of teachers on my world is the reason
I work in education. My cofounder, John Norlin, is a relentless
example of a life intentionally lived. My mentor,
Tyler Durman, is as honest and compassionate as he is tall.

My ex-partner, Harley, walked a long, weird, wonderful,
and winding road with me. We held many mirrors
up to each other, and I am forever grateful for that
adventure and where we've arrived on the far side.

The role of friendship continues to teach me everything
I need to know about how to do life better. Michael Zaro was my
"big brother" growing up as an only child, and from a young
age he taught me that you can be ridiculously cool *because* you are
consistently Kind. My current roommates—Esteban, Jackie,
Ben, and Jessie—help me dance and laugh and play more.
They remind me to be fully me and to show up in the world
with the full force of my gifts. To love and give of yourself fully—
that is perhaps the Kindest thing we can learn to do.

TABLE OF CONTENTS

PART 1	THE CASE FOR KINDNESS	1
Chapter 1	Kindness Isn't Normal	6
Chapter 2	Our Perspectives Drive Our Practices	8
Chapter 3	It's More Than Confetti	10

PART 2	LOOKING FOR ADVIL	15
Chapter 4	"The Empathy Gap"	18
Chapter 5	The Lonely Generation	21
Chapter 6	"A Culture of Personality"	23
Chapter 7	What Gets in the Way?	26

PART 3	INCOMPETENCE	31
Chapter 8	The Vocabulary of Kindness—More Than "Pretty Good"	37
Chapter 9	Emotional Regulation—Choosing How We Think	44
Chapter 10	Empathy—Standing in the Rain	52
Chapter 11	Vulnerability—The Courage to Care	62
Chapter 12	Forgiveness—People and Their Behaviors	70

PART 4	INSECURITY	81
Chapter 13	Rejection—Not-So-Free Hugs	88
Chapter 14	Failure—Elevators, Vultures, and the Terror of Not Doing It Right	95
Chapter 15	Embarrassment—To Dance When Everyone Is Watching	102
Chapter 16	Shame—The Scarcity of "Enough"	109

PART 5   INCONVENIENCE   115

Chapter 17   Busy—Making Time for Lunch Notes   122
Chapter 18   Exhaustion—Overconsumption and Overwhelm   129
Chapter 19   Fight Versus Feelings—Purpose Fuels Persistence   134

PART 6   CONSISTENCY   137

Chapter 20   Intersectional Thinking—Breaking Free from
             Chipotle Chicken Pasta   142

Conclusion   A Kinder World   155
Acknowledgments   161
Bibliography   163
Notes   165

1

[THE CASE FOR KINDNESS]

I call it the "Hot Dog Seat."

You know the one: the middle seat on airplanes where, for whatever number of necessary hours, you are trapped between two people "buns." The one where you have quiet battles for armrest space and a climate that is the average of whatever fan speed your neighbors have twisted to.

I found myself in the Hot Dog Seat early on in a speaking career that would take me to over six hundred campuses around the world talking to students about things like Kindness. This particular travel day was for a school that offered to fly me out to talk to their students. It was one of the first times a school put me on a plane, so I was humbled, nervous, and a bit exhausted. All I wanted to do was take a nap and prepare for the big day tomorrow. Helga, the woman who had just sat down next to me, had different plans.

I'd settled into my Hot Dog Seat before she arrived. As she pulled up to my row, she made it clear I didn't have to fully get into the aisle so she could get to her window seat, so we did the old middle school dance-off. You've been there: the stranger is passing by you in the small and contained area, you are standing to let them through, and suddenly you are face-to-face in a seventh-grade slow-dance pose.

Finally, she came to rest, and I immediately noted she had way more energy than I was hoping she would. She was fidgety and enthused. I was tired and wanted to take a nap. In my periphery, I saw that she had begun to decorate her space. A hand-knitted blanket. A dog trinket that hung from the seat-back pocket.

I suppose that, for a three-hour ride, you have to make it feel like home.

Despite my noise-canceling headphones, periphery-blinding neck pillow, and all other outward signs that I was ready to go to sleep, she tapped me on the shoulder to introduce herself.

"Hi, my name is Helga!"

Naptime officially delayed.

Without any sort of real conversational pause, she leaped into action. Helga asked me all kinds of questions: Where was I from, where was I going, what was I doing with my life . . . ?

I told her that I'm from Maine. I grew up in Seattle. I was on my way to go speak at a school—that's what I do with my life. She lit up. "Houston! I worked in a school as well! It was a high school. What was your favorite part of high school?"

"My senior year." My answers (and patience) were getting shorter.

"Why?" Her earnestness was insurmountable.

I explained that, during my last year of high school, some friends and I came together and created a group on campus called R.A.K.E., or Random Acts of Kindness, Etc. Once a week, we would meet and talk about Kindness. We shared why it was important, why the world needed more of it, and what we could do to exercise it. Then, we would go out onto our campus and practice! There were, I explained, only two rules to R.A.K.E.

1. MEET SOMEONE NEW

2. LEAVE THEM BETTER THAN YOU FOUND THEM

We realized that, at a school of our size (eighteen hundred students), we could meet someone new *every day* of high school and still not meet all the people in our building. We knew that everyone was craving some kind of connection, so we would talk often about what it looked like to effectively "leave someone better than we found them."

It wasn't long before Helga got emotional. She had hair that curled skyward and a smile that took in her whole face. She had green eyes that looked like they had their own gardens growing in them. She was wearing a cozy neck pillow that, based on all the evidence I'd gathered, didn't seem like it was going to be getting much use.

If you have the whole picture in your head, now picture her weeping.

Through her tears, she shared fervently that "there is nothing more important in the world than Kindness."

We probably all believe this sentiment on some level. But to Helga, it was a mantra rooted in pain.

She explained that the last time she had flown was three years ago. She had scrambled to an airport because she was woken up by a phone call from her dad's doctor. He told her to get to Arizona as quickly as possible because "Your dad's not doing very well."

Just as her plane was about to depart to Phoenix, the doctor called to inform her that her dad had passed away.

For the three-hour plane ride, she sat in stunned silence surrounded by strangers. When she arrived at the airport in Arizona, she stumbled to the nearest wall, crumpled to the ground, and wept.

And here is the part I'll never forget about Helga's story: for two hours, she sat and cried in the airport while nearly three thousand people walked by.

Not a single person stopped to help.

Chapter 1

KINDNESS ISN'T NORMAL

I spend a lot of time thinking about the importance of Kindness in a world seemingly too busy for it. Kindness is one of these essential things that we collectively say is good, but we collectively aren't very good at.

Why? Why are we so bad at something we believe in?

Why is it that we can so universally agree on the value of something and not be very skilled at it? How can Helga sit in pain, alone in an airport, and have three thousand people bypass her suffering?

This book, in many ways, is for Helga. Almost every day I think or talk about her story. In some ways it's because I know that, at any given moment, I could live her story. I'm acutely aware that none of us are immune from adversity. We will all, at some point along the way, be desperate for a moment of human Kindness and connection.

For two hours, three thousand strangers walked by her moment of profound hurt. In her deepest sadness and loneliness, thousands of opportunities for companionship and comfort shuffled or sprinted by on their own well-intentioned way.

I was in the Hot Dog Seat, crying while she cried, when she arrived at her conclusion: "You know what I realized as three thousand people walked by, Houston? I realized that Kindness isn't normal."

Kindness isn't normal.

Those words have stuck with me all these years. It has been the foundation upon which I've built much of what I do, because I want to live in a world where Kindness is the baseline—a world where everyone is capable of meeting the basic human need for attention, hopefulness, and care. A world where people have the skills and the courage to stop and help someone crying in the airport. A world that believes in Kindness as the single most important skill for more meaningful lives and more abundant, caring, connected communities.

I believe in a world where Kindness is *normal*. And I've learned along the way that it's going to take a lot of work.

Chapter 2

OUR PERSPECTIVES DRIVE OUR PRACTICES

$\mathcal{I}$ grew up trying to memorize the longest words I could find. I remember being in the bathtub at age six trying to learn how to spell "temperature." My mom would patiently break the word apart: tem·per·a·ture.

I would scour the internet to see if I could find bigger and sillier spelling challenges. When I was eleven, I tackled "pneumonoultramicroscopicsilicovolcanoconiosis." Before you start a not-so-quick Google search (it takes a minute just to type it), I'll fill you in on its meaning: it's a lung disease caused by the inhalation of fine silica or quartz dust. It's the longest English word on the market at forty-five letters, and I spent a full forty-eight hours trying to memorize it.

Maybe it was just my only-child desire to win at all things, but even beyond winning, I've always been drawn to the power of words. "Language and the Brain" describes language as one of the primary ways that we understand the world around us.[1] It plays a starring and widespread role in the human brain, aiding in everything from processing color to making moral judgments. It dictates how we construct and remember events, categorize objects, process smells and sounds, think about time, do mental math, and experience and express emotions. You get the point. Words are kind of a big deal.

Much of our understanding of language is taught to us through experience. Which means, if we aren't paying attention, our ultimately narrowlaned, individual life experiences can inform how we define many words that control much of our life. Our siloed, independent experiences aren't always the most trustworthy source of definitions for things that affect us interdependently. As an example, if our experience growing up with the word "love" is shaped by a series of failed or abusive relationships with the adults we trust, we will begin to think about (or even fear) love in ways that are unique to those experiences. If we grow up in a household where Kindness looks like two parents who make our dinner each night and sit down for a family meal, we may have a hard time understanding someone who comes from a single-grandparent home where Kindness looks like someone remembering to leave some leftovers in the fridge.

No perspective is inherently wrong. However, if we don't have the tools to reflect on how our experiences have defined these words in our lives, then we become the victim of hand-me-down definitions. That is to say, we accept the definition our lives have offered to us instead of wrestling with any possibility of the word meaning something more.

The way we think about things in our brain shapes the way we interact with them in the world. Words (and our definitions of them) shape nearly everything we do.

So what is your definition of Kindness? And perhaps the more important question: How does your definition of Kindness shape the way you interact with it in the world?

Chapter 3

IT'S MORE THAN CONFETTI

W e are talking about Kindness more than ever before. While interpersonal conversations are one element of this chatter, our culture currently speaks loudest through products and posts. Target has a whole Kindness T-shirt line. There are hashtags focused on happiness. There are a plethora of Pinterest-y posters promoting positivity. Brands are popping up with mottoes focused on doing or being good. Nearly every school I have ever worked with incorporates Kindness into their motto, mantra, or mission.

But *how* we talk about something is even more important than the *frequency* with which we talk about it.

I've worked with over six hundred schools around the world, and one of the most common Kindness posters I've seen in these schools reads like this:

> "Throw Kindness around like confetti!"

I want to gently tear this poster down from the internet and the hallways.

Don't get me wrong; it's well-intentioned. The quote is simply asking us to be more liberal in how we spread and share our Kindness. And certainly the world needs more of it!

But I believe that if Kindness were as simple or as easy as confetti, the world would be a much Kinder place.

In fact, quotes like this one (and many others in schools or online) talk about Kindness in a similarly well-intentioned, cute, and playful way.

"Just be Kind!"

"Kindness is free. Sprinkle that stuff everywhere."

And while they make for great products and posters, they can do more harm than good. Without paying proper attention, we've started to "fluffify" the thing. We are talking about Kindness in an oversimplified way.

One of the biggest barriers to a Kinder world is the way we speak about Kindness. When we make something *sound* easy, we don't allocate the necessary resources, energy, or time to actually improve at it. The kind of Kindness the world needs isn't being accurately portrayed, let alone taught. As a result, there is a glaring delta between perceived importance and actual action.

What if we talked about Kindness in a way that honored how hard it is? What if we taught skills in our education system that supported the challenging and messy work of Deep Kindness in our lives?

Deep Kindness. Not Confetti Kindness.

Simple and confetti-like actions of Kindness are a piece of the puzzle, but they aren't the whole picture.

Clearly outlining the differences between these concepts is what this book is all about. It's about offering a more thoughtful vocabulary for the critically important concept of Kindness.

Here are a few types that may come up:

- **COMMON KINDNESS:**

  "Please" and "Thank you." Politeness and pleasantries. While certainly important and demonstrative of basic respect for others, these acts of Kindness aren't necessarily changing anyone's world. They keep the gears turning, but sometimes fail to acknowledge the bigger, broken machine.

- **CONFETTI KINDNESS:**

  The mass-marketed, feel-good Kindness that I associate with bright colors, poppy news stories, and warm fuzzies like Pay-It-Forward coffee lines or other random acts.

Let me be clear from the start: I believe that both of these first two Kindnesses are critical in a world craving gentleness and optimism. This book does not dismiss Confetti Kindness as outright wrong or bad—these actions of fun or generosity provide hope that people are doing good in a world that can sometimes feel bleak. Almost always, they are rooted in good intentions and delivered in an earnest attempt to help. There is nothing inherently wrong with Confetti Kindness, but there is a more profound category of care that the world desperately needs.

- **DEEP KINDNESS:**
The kind of Kindness that overcomes selfishness and fear. The sort of generosity that expects nothing in return. The unconditional care that is given despite a person's shortcomings or ugliness. The commitment to consistent, thoughtful action that proves, over time, that your giving is not dependent on circumstance or convenience. Deep Kindness requires something more than politeness or even an honest desire to help—it requires careful self-reflection, profound courage, a willingness to be humbled, and hard-earned social and emotional skills. Deep Kindness is the by-product of a whole lot of emotional intelligences coming together in concert to perform an action that may look externally simple but is quite internally complicated. It's the kind that overcomes generational hate and champions justice. It's the type of Kindness we must teach (and explore for ourselves) if we are ever going to live in a world that is less divisive and more compassionate. It's the kind of Kindness that stops to help Helga.

If most of what we've heard or seen growing up is reductionistic one-liners such as "be kind" or cutesy commands like "sprinkle that stuff everywhere because it's free," then we will continue to reduce this beautiful and complicated idea of Kindness down to simple sayings, Post-it Note pleasantries, and high fives in hallways.

There are plenty of books available that can offer stories and ideas for Confetti Kindness, and I urge you to read them and enjoy! I would never dismiss the value of these small and powerful moments that can encourage a smile, change a day, or inspire a movement. But this book is more interested in unpacking things that can feel a little bit uglier and perhaps a little less fun. It will feel prickly and uncomfortable at times, and that is a good thing. We'll never find new answers if we keep asking the old questions. I want to explore the limits of our compassion and understand what's required for us to live in the Kindest version of this world.

The practice of Deep Kindness doesn't happen just because we believe in Kindness. It's something to strive toward, and a skill set that has infinite room for improvement. It's also not exclusive of Common Kindness or Confetti Kindness. In fact, the two of them are foundational for the ongoing work of Deep Kindness. The consistent and thoughtful exercise of Common Kindness and Confetti Kindness helps you take a perspective rooted in respect, cultivate meaningful habits, get the "small wins" that drive you toward bigger ones, and strengthen the necessary muscle of courage to set you up for scary action when Kindness matters most.

To use the body as a metaphor, Common Kindness is knowing why working out is important and getting your steps in when you can. Confetti Kindness is taking a Pilates class with a friend or getting a run in when it works with your schedule. Deep Kindness is the culmination of years of thoughtful nutrition and habitual exercise that results in ongoing health, wellness, and real physical transformation. One *can* lead to the other, but it doesn't happen by accident. To move from one to the other is predicated on understanding, action, and discipline over time. It's hard work, but the rewards are profound.

In order to demonstrate this kind of Kindness, it is important that you understand the skills necessary to get there.

Deep Kindness requires *empathy* and *perspective-taking*. How am I supposed to give you something you *truly need* if I don't attempt to understand what you need first?

Deep Kindness requires *resilience*. Do you know how much fortitude it takes to offer Kindness, get rejected, hurt, or laughed at, and return to give Kindness again? Grit is necessary for unconditional love in the face of adversity, cruelty, or conditions that would more naturally lend themselves to hate.

Deep Kindness requires *courage*. The willingness to take great risk at personal cost, and expose yourself to judgment, mockery, or failure in order to demonstrate that you care. To extend your own ego to the wolves, knowing that perhaps there is someone who needs you on the far side of fear.

Deep Kindness requires *forgiveness*. It asks us to see others through the generous perspective of hope, and to believe that people are capable of growth. The unforgiving person sees others (and sometimes themselves) as incapable of change. Lifelong grudges are held because one or both parties stubbornly cling to the narrative "They meant to hurt me and always will."

Tom Hanks's famous line from *A League of Their Own* resonates here: "It's supposed to be hard. If it wasn't hard, everyone would do it. The hard is what makes it great." The challenge of Deep Kindness is what makes it so worthwhile, life-shaping, and world-changing. If we are going to improve at it effectively, we have to talk about it in a way that celebrates its complexity and honors its hardness.

What if the poster we grew up with said something like this:

> "Throw Kindness around like it's the most important and meaningful resource we have."

That'd be a poster worth hanging. And that's the kind of Kindness this book is about.

2

[LOOKING FOR ADVIL]

*P*eople more actively seek Advil than vitamins. We more readily look for things to alleviate pain than pursue practices that reduce pain in the first place. We are reactive by nature, and it is far too often that we find post-trauma clarity in what "could have been done."

Unfortunately, our culture considers Kindness a nice-to-have rather than a nonnegotiable. It's the icing on top, but it's not the whole cake.

We need to understand the hurt we can (and must!) address through Deep Kindness. While I wish Kindness were a vitamin, we are actively in pain and need something stronger. We need revelation, transformation, and some extra-strength Advil.

We're in need of a more compelling case for Kindness than its cuteness. We must be able to recognize Kindness as the single most important ingredient for a healthy, connected, and conscious world. Kindness is not the Band-Aid. It's the cure.

The following pages will outline, in devastating detail, why our world needs pain relief. Now.

Chapter 4

"THE EMPATHY GAP"

T he American Psychological Association (APA) revealed the average student today has as much anxiety as the average psychiatric patient from the 1950s.[1] Anxiety is increasing in our world, and there are hundreds of reasons that contribute to this amplification of worry. To start, our brains aren't really designed for the daily deluge of data they receive. "Time Flies" suggests American adults spend over eleven hours per day listening to, watching, reading, or interacting with media.[2] The research out of the University of California San Diego tells us that we are exposed to about thirty-four gigabytes of information a day, including over 105,000 words, in our waking hours.[3] It is an overwhelm of information that is un-curated and un-processable.

What happens when most of the content we are digesting is digital and impersonal? What happens when our brains are being bombarded by pixels instead of people? Well, the evidence is in our interactions. A study out of the University of Michigan tells us that empathy has dropped 40 percent in college-aged students since the year 2000.[4] That sharp decline in our ability to show empathy pairs serendipitously with various tech inventions and advancements.

It is a humbling reminder that, while we are more digitally connected than ever, we are also more isolated and anxious. For the millennials who grew up during this era of technological innovation in social networking, we have found ourselves unexpectedly lonely.

I got my first cell phone in eighth grade and remember fondly the advanced game of black-and-white *Snake* that I played. I remember being enthralled by *Brick Breaker* on the BlackBerry and the deep desire to know everyone's PIN number so I could BlackBerry Messenger them. I remember the iPhone's glassy aesthetic and an app store that revealed unlimited possibilities.

Unfortunately, there will always be similar examples of things that simultaneously delight us, while demanding our most valuable currency: attention.

Today, not much has changed. Most of us have witnessed the modern reality of eating dinner as a family: everyone at the table has their faces in their phones and out of the conversation.

Who, over time, do you think will win the battle for our attention: The devices that refresh relentlessly and are programmed to tap into our habits and happiness? Or the person in front of us who is rather imperfect and sometimes disagreeable? There is a reason that science fiction novels often warn us that, if we aren't conscious and careful, machines could control most of our daily life. Ultimately, apps are easier to deal with than attitudes.

Who wouldn't want to reveal to others only the most curated and celebratory parts of their lives? What if the only way we knew each other was through our most popular posts and photo shoots? If I have the option to share with the masses only my most well-lit and well-groomed angles—only my most well-distilled and well-written thoughts—it seems reasonable to spend most of my time cultivating that carefully crafted version of me.

Our profiles provide our most prepackaged personas and, as we browse the catalogs of people on our social media, we are given VIP access to brutal false comparisons. "I wish my hair looked like that!" or "I want my relationship to be like theirs" is the conscious or unconscious internal dialogue that compares the fullness of our personhood with a fraction of another's perfectly planned photo shoot.

And what happens when the dopamine hits and data bits are readily available at our fingertips? They become the first things we reach for when we have a "spare moment." My personal desire to reach for my device has gotten so bad that I've started getting the phantom buzzes—those false rings in my pocket that let my brain pretend that now is a good time to check the phone because it's probably, almost certainly, nearly definitely something important and urgent.

And why sit in a moment of stillness, silence, or (God forbid!) *boredom*, when you can have the world's information and interconnectedness in your hands?

Neuroscience tells us that it is actually moments of boredom where empathy and creativity are cultivated. *Greater Good Magazine* argues that the in-between moments of silence, pause, or stillness when we get to daydream—a necessary vacuum of the clamor and clutter—are the empty canvas we create from.[5] In our current reality, we don't have time to be bored. There is too much content to consume, friends to message, and stories to tell.

This is nothing new. Researchers studied how television affected creativity and imagination—key ingredients of empathy—in Canada in the 1980s.[6] They discovered that, as soon as TVs were introduced into communities, there was a reduction in divergent thinking skills and imagination. Today, we have the most powerful TVs we could dream of in our pockets.

We have more access to content than ever before, and the direct by-product is more anxiety. Whether it's information overload, the lose-lose comparison game, or the inability to be bored, our culture is careening away from connection (no matter how much we think we are creating it).

Here's the tough part: Dr. Michele Borba, in her book *Unselfie*, says that when anxiety increases, empathy decreases. She calls it the "Empathy Gap," and she builds a strong case that it is widening. It's really cause and effect: the more worried I am about what's going on in my life, the harder a time I will have worrying about what's going on in yours.

THE KIND OF KINDNESS THE WORLD NEEDS . . .

is one that starts with understanding. It's the kind that willingly climbs the mountain that is anxiety and knows that connection is cultivated, not clicked on. It's the kind that realizes that Kindness isn't a "nice-to-have," but a "must-have." Perhaps it's not a supplement or a pain reliever at all, but rather a fundamentally key ingredient in helping heal a deeply wounded world.

Chapter 5

THE LONELY GENERATION

I've spent a lot of nights in Hampton Inns. The less glamorous parts of the work of a "motivational speaker" are the many late-night rental car shuttles and the rather frequent dinners-for-one. In 2016 alone, I worked with over 130 schools or conferences around the country and was hitting my stride professionally. My mom had also recently been diagnosed with Stage IV colon cancer, my marriage was struggling, and I had almost zero friends near my new home in Los Angeles.

My most "successful" year of speaking was also the loneliest year of my life.

Ironically, I'm not alone in this loneliness. In 2018, a survey completed by Cigna and Ipsos that included twenty thousand U.S. adults ages eighteen and older stated that 40 percent of respondents reported feeling alone and 47 percent reported feeling left out. One in four felt like they were not understood, and nearly half felt like their relationships were not meaningful and said they often felt isolated. At the core of this data, they discovered the primary cause was a lack of significant human connectedness.[1]

While some cultures would tout independence as the disposition of the successful, they don't always provide the necessary caveats about connection. When we focus too much on independence, we subtly dismiss the critical need to be able to work in teams, be a part of a community, collaborate on big problems, and ask for help. When we are independent but not connected, we can quickly find ourselves successful but not supported.

And what happens next? Well, as you can imagine, that isolation can lead to loneliness, and that loneliness is associated with depression and suicide. Someone feeling socially isolated may become depressed. Someone who is depressed may shut themselves off from friends and family and increase that sense of social isolation. This is a vicious cycle, and you've almost certainly seen someone in it or been in it yourself.

According to the APA, when we are lonely, we are at higher risk for:

- Cognitive decline
- Alzheimer's disease
- Cardiovascular disease
- Cancer
- Inflammatory disease

All this data compiles into this stunning fact: loneliness will reduce your lifespan as much as smoking fifteen cigarettes a day.[2]

These things affect us all, from a dinner-for-one at your nearest Hampton Inn to the unvisited senior citizen in the nursing home. The most dramatic increase is in our youngest population. *Psychology Today* argues Generation Z is, quantifiably, the loneliest generation.[3] The by-product? Suicide overtook homicide as the number two killer of teenagers.

Let's not dwell here too long. We collectively see the problem: we live in a more digitally connected and socially isolated world than ever before. Loneliness has doubled over the past few decades despite a thousand pieces of technology and innovations that "make us more connected than ever before."

I know the distinct feeling of scrolling on my phone, late at night, looking at pictures of friends while I lay my lonely head to rest on a stiff, white hotel pillow. My Diamond status awards me two bottles of water, but I'm only drinking for one.

THE KIND OF KINDNESS THE WORLD NEEDS . . .
is one that helps us feel less alone.

Chapter 6

"A CULTURE OF PERSONALITY"

*H*ave you ever been really disappointed to meet someone in real life? A hero on a screen or in magazines but, when you meet them, nothing you admired about them from afar lines up with their actions in front of you?

Susan Cain, in her book *Quiet: The Power of Introverts in a World That Can't Stop Talking*, does this little experiment where she flips through self-help books from one hundred years ago and finds the most commonly used titles and words. At that time in history, the frequent fliers were words like "honor," "humility," "courage," and "character."

She completed the same experiment with self-help books from today and found words like "charisma," "charm," "funny," and "popular." Why the change? One possible reason that Cain suggests is the one-hundred-year shift from agricultural farming to big business—a shift from people working next to people they've known their whole lives to working in big cities with strangers they must impress.

She writes that we've shifted from a culture of character to a culture of personality.

It seems subtle, but it's actually a radical and seismic societal shift. A culture of character says, "How do I improve myself so that I can serve my community and my world?" A culture of character is interested in moral pursuits and integrity. Cain tells us it's a culture that makes room for the introvert and the extrovert.

Today, we have a culture of personality. A culture that says, "How do I improve myself so that I can serve my reputation, my brand, my followers . . . me?" We have a culture that values whoever is loudest in the room. The one who makes the most noise and gets the best results. During this shift, movie stars became the ultimate role models, followed a few decades later by the rise of the Influencer and the YouTuber. People who generate attention become the most worthy of our collective eyeballs. And so the question naturally becomes: What do I need to do to get attention?

In the competition between do-gooding and drama, unfortunately, Kindness loses. We seem to be more attracted to a mess than to a message.

Personality and character. The distinction between the two words feels important: you give the average personality test to Martin Luther King Jr. and Hitler and they are going to score very similarly—they both had big vision, thought strategically about systematic change, and were brilliant orators. The critical, culture-defining difference? Their character.

Research tells us that our dominant personality traits are more or less set by the age of seven.[1] We kind of come shipped with them. Character, on the other hand, is shaped by the choices we make every day. Hitler chose to use his gifts to hurt, while Martin Luther King Jr. fought for hope—and the results shaped history forever. The average person makes thirty-five thousand choices each day, and every one of them, big and small, can shape our ability to be kind, patient, and committed people. Character is a habit.

Let's put it into practice. Someone might say, "I just tell people how it is. That's my personality!" To which I might say, "No, your personality might be that you are assertive. But your character right now shows that you are being a jerk."

It is possible to be assertive in a way that is Kind and loving. We decide how we use our personality and gifts to help or hurt others. Those choices are choices of character.

My brain works in metaphors, so I think about it like this: Personality is what we prefer to wear to the gym. Character is how hard we work out.

Have you ever seen someone who looks really good at the gym, but they aren't very sweaty? Have you ever known people who are charming but not always very Kind behind closed doors? People who are funny, but that humor is usually at the expense of others (especially those who have less power than them)? People who are charismatic enough to get themselves elected or selected into positions of power, but don't really want to do the work?

These are examples of people with a lot of personality, but not very much character. The difference between the two is important. A culture rich with personality but low on character is a dangerous one.

THE KIND OF KINDNESS THE WORLD NEEDS . . .

is rooted in a desire for the common good. It's the kind willing to get sweaty in pursuit of selflessness and do the hard work necessary to cultivate their character—their habits—toward compassion.

Chapter 7

WHAT GETS IN THE WAY?

I was speaking to an audience filled with people who had seen me before. Some people in the audience had probably seen me five times. Gigs like this always force creativity to come forward, as there is something distinctly less-than-inspirational about seeing a speaker share the same stories on repeat.

My time slot was third in the day for a student-driven leadership conference that brought in five thousand young people from around Washington State. My talk was to follow Noémi Ban, a ninety-four-year-old Holocaust survivor. A rather tough act to follow in more ways than one.

She was brilliant. At the age of twenty-two, Ban was sent to Auschwitz alongside eleven of her relatives who did not make it out of that horrific camp alive. Ban was later sent to Buchenwald concentration camp, where she intentionally constructed faulty bombs to save future, unknown lives. She escaped during a death march and found her way back home to Hungary.

After becoming a teacher, Ban again found herself trapped. During the time of the Soviet oppression, she tried to escape to Austria. After one failed attempt, she tried again and made it out successfully by sneaking across the border in a shipment of giant balls of yarn. You can't make this stuff up.

During the entirety of her talk, she had a glass of water in front of her. She shared stories of how the Nazis would taunt their captives with water after starving and dehydrating them for days. They wanted the Jews to attack each other, proving that they were "animals."

At the end of her talk, she held the glass aloft, sipped, and spoke her final line: "Freedom."

I still get teary-eyed thinking of Noémi's heroic journey. She made her way slowly off the stage, and I felt like my whole brain had been reprogrammed by Noémi's narrative. It was my turn to talk, and I realized that up until that point—for the previous seven years—I'd been trying to sell my audiences on the idea of Kindness. I thought that if I could just convince them of its worthiness, everyone would show it more and practice it better. If I could sell people on its inherent worth, the world would be a Kinder place.

Listening to Noémi, I realized that I'd been selling answers when what I needed to do was ask better questions. Perhaps the more meaningful and challenging call to action about Kindness had less to do with its implied morality and more to do with our willingness (and ability) to ask ourselves the question, "What gets in the way?"

We already know the value of Kindness. We all already believe in the idea of the thing and want more of it in our lives and in the world. Everyone, fundamentally and humanly, craves compassion. And yet, we are capable of the Holocaust. We are capable of a world wrought with homelessness. We are capable of food abundance living next door to starvation. We are capable of walking by someone hurting in the airport.

How can we so collectively believe in Kindness yet be so collectively bad at it?

There is an observable gap in our current culture between what we know is good and what we are actually good at. In that gap resides both the world's sufferings and our most personal heartaches. The widening gap between moral knowing and Kind action is a quiet epidemic that many will diagnose in others, but few will treat in themselves. It is a disease that drives us toward loneliness, greed, anguish, and a deep separateness that prevents us from solving the most pressing needs of our collective future.

Maria Popova at Brain Pickings wrote about the Greek term *akrasia*, which is used to describe our "weakness of will."[1] It is a term to reference our generationally unbroken habit of not listening to what we *know* should be heard. It alludes to our repetitive failure to take action on things we *know* are Right with a capital "R." Akrasia causes us to simultaneously understand what we *should* do but rather frustratingly choose *not* to do. We've all been in a moment where we could identify a need and decided not to meet it.

How can I better mind my own gap? I started asking myself, "Why wouldn't I stop and help Helga?" In all those small ways I have dismissed Kindness in my life—those simple moments where I walked by situations and knew I could have done something—why did I not practice this thing that I believe in? That I'd have wanted for myself if the tables were turned?

Of course, there are occasionally very legitimate reasons for not pausing to help someone like Helga. You could be late for a connecting flight en route to visit someone sick in your family. You may have an important event you need to be on time for and are already running late. Perhaps you truly don't feel physically or emotionally safe in the given circumstance.

Situations like this are the exception, not the norm. Most of the time, people will pass by opportunities for Kindness for one of three main reasons:

1. **INCOMPETENCE:** When I don't know *how* to do a thing, I tend to avoid that thing. The gym is a good example for me: there are so many machines in that place that I have zero understanding of, so I tend to relegate myself to a familiar three exercises. Kindness is similar. If the action of Kindness requires a skill that I'm not very skilled at (yet), then I'll typically avoid that action or exercise and do what feels comfortable. For example, if I am not very skilled at empathy, I may not feel capable of stopping to hear about Helga's hurt.

2. **INSECURITY:** When I'm *afraid* of a thing, sometimes I avoid that thing. Every compassionate action we take exposes us to a variety of risks like being judged, embarrassed,

dismissed, or laughed at, or feeling like a failure. The most frustratingly near-direct correlation is this: the more you care, the more likely you are to get hurt. You can't invest in passion without risking some level of pain. If I am worried about failing Helga (or being judged by other people walking by), I may be too scared to stop and engage with her.

3. **INCONVENIENCE:** If I don't *feel* like doing a thing, sometimes I avoid that thing. On any given day, we might feel tired, busy, overworked, hurt, hungry . . . or any number of other human emotions that actually make Kindness harder. These daily inconveniences (paired with our never-ending to-do lists) can keep us practicing the Common Kindnesses that are more passive politenesses than proactive pursuits. If I am feeling overwhelmed by what's happening in my world, dealing with Helga is simply something I don't have time for.

As I reflect on my own answer to, "What gets in the way?" I've realized that my main categorical barriers all have something in common. They all start with the same letter and, more important, the primary identity of our biggest obstacle: *I*.

There is a popular story about the London publication of *The Times*. It is said they printed an open question to their readers: "What is wrong with the world?" It is a question I am sure we all have many answers for in our current reality. I imagine you could write a long-winded essay or deliver an earnest speech on the subject.

In the early 1900s, however, the prolific writer and philosopher G. K. Chesterton had a much more direct approach. He wrote back simply, "I am. Sincerely, G. K. Chesterton."

The story is a great summary of our biggest challenge when it comes to Kindness; the only person that would prevent me from stopping to help

Helga that day in the airport is me. *I* am my number one obstacle to overcome when it comes to practicing Kindness.

Kindness, then, is often about getting ourselves out of the way.

It is important to note that, like all of life, Kindness is a balancing act. There are some days where the barriers are simply insurmountable, or the risk is just too high. There are some opportunities for Kindness that are better served by other people and it may instead be your job to empower *them* to step up. With certainty, there will also be days where you will be the one in need of Kindness, in which case the Kindest thing you can do is ask for help and practice receiving the help that is offered.

Just like going to the gym, we will all move at different paces and utilize different workout programs. Our exercises should be designed to meet us at our current ability, while challenging us enough to get us to our goals.

My goals are big. I want a world where Kindness is commonplace.

Not Confetti Kindness, but Deep Kindness. The kind of Kindness that demands a better world than the one Noémi had. The kind that doesn't give lip service to the words "Liberty and Justice for All," but actually mobilizes the resources and practices to arrive there.

The next time you see a glass of water, I hope you think of Noémi. May this basic and everyday convenience we take for granted remind you of this pervasive and quintessential human need that we all have to be *free*. And may that spur you into a lifestyle of action that demands a higher level of Kindness than what is common or confetti-like.

Deep Kindness requires the messiest type of work—the kind that acknowledges that I am both the root of the problem *and* the potential source of the solution.

We must embrace that mess to *Make Kindness Normal.*

3

[INCOMPETENCE]

A few years ago I sat down with Justin Baldoni to talk about empathy. Justin is a thoughtful actor and activist who creates content that leverages his influence for good. He has helped create an online series about masculinity, directed a movie that champions the cystic fibrosis community, and hosts annual events on LA's Skid Row, where he brings resources, music, and people together for an event rooted in humanization and connection.

One of the things he shared during our conversation is that the word "human" in Arabic translates roughly to "to forget." We spent some time unpacking the idea that perhaps we are born with everything we need to live a meaningful, Kind life and that, along the way, our world or culture forces us *to forget*. The conscious life, then, isn't so much about learning as it is remembering. Or maybe just paying closer attention to something that is already there but is hard to find. I sometimes imagine enlightenment as returning home from a lifetime of global treasure-hunting to discover that a pile of jewels is buried in your garden box near the tomatoes.

I bear witness to young wisdom all the time. While my four-year-old neighbor occasionally wrestles with selfishness and emotional outbursts, most of his innate programming is actually quite open, curious, empathetic, and Kind. He knows when I'm having a bad day, is wildly accepting of every kid in his preschool class, and wants to invite his friend Ansel over all the time so he can share his newest toy.

My little neighbor friend exists with little judgment toward himself or others. He paints abstract pictures and dedicates them in my honor. He smiles when I smile and gets concerned when I'm sad.

All these things he will, without careful attention, grow out of until he makes a conscious decision to grow back into them.

Are we born fully competent at all the skills necessary for a fully compassionate life? I'm not sure I'd go that far. But are we born with a predisposition toward openness, learning, creativity, invitation, adventure, and care? Absolutely.

But then we have to get all "human" and forget.

Perhaps this resonates with you on a philosophical level or a spiritual one. I love these abstractions and metaphors—they help me to build a multidimensional understanding of the richly complicated pursuit of a Kinder life.

On a more practical level, however, perhaps we could all agree that most skills in our life simply require hard work. Blood, sweat, and tears. Hopefully some smiles in there, too.

Meditation and metaphors are a piece of the puzzle for some, but there is no way around the disciplined pursuit of key emotional and social competencies. Empathy is a skill that we can improve throughout our whole life. And it's not a passive pursuit. It's not a cross-my-fingers-and-hope-I-get-better-at-it kind of thing. It's not a coming-of-age ceremony where you are endowed with improved listening skills and more effective perspective-taking. It is a conscious and rigorous pursuit, over time, through structured and unstructured practice that improves our empathetic abilities (and lots of other skills like it that are foundational to the practice of Kindness).

Let's return to the gym metaphor, since building our relational muscles has many parallels to building our physical ones. When I walk into the gym (we are speaking in hypotheticals here, as I'm not at the gym very often), I am confronted with one hundred different space-age contraptions that work out muscles both familiar and alien. Just because it's my personal reality, let's paint an even more vivid picture. The gym closest to me in Venice, California, is one of the original Gold's Gym establishments. It's referred to as the Mecca of Bodybuilding. Arnold Schwarzenegger, the literal Terminator, works out there weekly.

So there I am, in my loose-fitting "muscle tee" that seems to be having the opposite visual effect, staring down foreign-looking machines filled with fitness models and heavyweight legends.

If nothing else, just going to my gym is an exercise in humility.

Now, here is the key question and how this whole metaphor relates to "What gets in the way?"

> When presented with one hundred machines, which ones are you most likely to use: The three you've used before or the ninety-seven you haven't?

We tend to gravitate toward what we know. If we are not as familiar with a machine, our most natural human tendency is to head toward one that makes sense to us. If we don't have a coach or a friend teaching us how to use the new machine, then our instincts want to keep us comfortable.

There are competencies related to Kindness that are necessary for the action of Kindness. If you are missing any of those skills—if you are ill-equipped in empathy, for example—you are way less likely to stop and help Helga.

Why? Well, she doesn't need a Post-it Note or confetti. She needs someone to hurt alongside her. To be present to her suffering and empathize with her. To listen or simply hold space for her. To call a professional or offer a shoulder to cry on (and to be able to diagnose when one is needed over the other).

If you are not so good (consciously or unconsciously) at accessing your own hurt or listening without jumping in with advice, then you'll probably opt out of the experience altogether. You will walk on by Helga in the airport even if you believe fully in Kindness.

When we avoid one exercise, we give energy to another. One of the most pervasive issues of our phones is that the more we become comfortable and skilled at online interaction, the more we will choose that option when "connecting." For most of us, we'd rather delve into the digital while standing in line or walking down the street than engage with the strangers around us. And, through repetition, we increase our muscles in one space while reducing them in another.

What are the skills that we, as humans, need to *remember* in order to be effective in our Kindness? What skills do we need to be taught to be capable of a Kinder life? What muscles do we need to exercise, even when it's out of our routine or wildly uncomfortable, to be strong enough for a moment like stopping to help Helga?

It's not that we don't want to be Kind. Perhaps we actually don't know how.

Chapter 8

THE VOCABULARY OF KINDNESS— MORE THAN "PRETTY GOOD"

I had just finished speaking at a high school near Los Angeles. It was back-to-back assemblies in a massive, double-wide, double-sided gym. The projectors displayed images on both of the too-small central screens that seemed as if they were in their digital death throes.

I gave it my all, as you have to do in these situations. The average high school crowd doesn't really care about who you are, where you came from, or what gig you did yesterday. They are in bumpy bleachers, their butts already hurting, with all the world's information at their fingertips. If you don't say something worthwhile in the first thirty seconds, phones come out quickly and you're in for a long, listen-less experience. Times two thousand.

So, I dove right in. I was talking about the Hot Dog Seat and the gap between what we know is good and what we are good at. With a bit of frenetic energy, I went from the left to the right sides of the gym and I shared my hope that we "haven't maxed out on Kindness in our world." I offered my plea for us to "be better at being better to each other."

Some of the audience was getting on board. Some of them were just bored. Ten years into this, you start to develop a quick sense of how many teammates you have early on. This generation is exposed to a lot of scary and overwhelming information every day. They see corrupt decisions that serve older generations more than theirs and they experience the second-hand smoke of many of the world's messes being made. So when I drum up support for a more compassionate world, most of them start to nod their heads. You'd be encouraged by their enthusiasm when you tap the right vein.

A bit sweaty and a little exhausted, I finished my second assembly. Most students have been programmed to get up and get back into the grind as they file their meandering way out of the gym and on to the next class. Many of them had already forgotten about 90 percent of what I'd just shared—a statistic with which I've had to come to terms with. They get plenty of data every day, and there is no guarantee that my stories will stick for much longer than the moment in which I'm sharing them.

But there are almost always a few. The few who, for whatever reason, needed some of the perspectives that I shared that day. The people who were on the precipice of something, and what I offered in that assembly pushed them toward or away from whatever they were navigating, in a way that they needed to hear.

And some of them, standing in a line in front of me, just need someone to listen.

Call it serendipity, synchronicity, or something more. Whatever larger power brings my story intersecting with theirs at the right moment is something that I am grateful for—these small moments are the biggest wins of my work.

I had spent about ten minutes chatting with different students when this kid with long hair and a low backpack walked up. In a slow and deliberate way, as if he was putting on an outfit he'd rarely worn, he said, "Hey, man. My friend said you were boring, but he must not have been listening. I thought you were pretty good."

I could have done without the whole first half of that compliment.

And the second part? Did this kid just wait in line to tell me that I was "pretty good"?

We don't need to dive into all my childhood insecurities (yet) about me being good enough or using high achievementism as my primary pathway to lovability. Needless to say, a backhanded compliment like this was simultaneously sweet and a little bit haunting.

My insecurity started spinning: Why did this kid's friend think I was boring? How many other kids thought I was boring? Am I, now ten years into this, losing my touch? Why did this kid wait around to basically tell me I was average?

Self-doubt isn't a hole in the ground that you fall into. It's a ladder that plummets to an unknown depth, and for some reason, in spite of the darkness and the sense of horror you get when looking down, you have to find out what's at the bottom. So, rung by rung, you keep descending.

In reflecting on this moment for many months afterward, I've found my way out of the pit. With some optimistic clarity, I've come to the conclusion that perhaps this was actually the Kindest thing this kid knew how to say.

One of the many ways we can give and receive Kindness is through compliments, affirmations, or appreciations. There is a whole vocabulary to this practice. The skill of Kind Communication is not often talked about or taught; compliments are usually passed off as fluffy, so we've contented ourselves with the most commonplace of catchphrases, like "You look so nice!" or "Thanks for your service."

I would contest that the communication skills needed to tell someone they have a nice sweater are wildly different than the ones required to tell a person about the impact they've had on your career or life. The vocabulary necessary to compliment someone's smile is quite different from the words required to eulogize a life. Knowing what to say in the right situations, with the right words, *and* in a way that allows people to receive them . . . well, it can be a big deal.

In some situations, it is life or death.

I don't need to regale you with stories of people's lives who have been saved by Kind words, but we can all imagine ourselves or someone in our circle who has been told something that they hold very dear to them. A proper compliment at a critical time can be a benchmark moment in how we view ourselves.

Sometimes words, or rather the memory of them, are a life raft when everything else seems hell-bent on sinking us.

If I don't know *what to say* to Helga, I am more likely to avoid engaging with her altogether. No one likes the sensation of speechlessness (unless it's in response to something beautiful or awe-inspiring). When our closest friends or family members share something hard, there is something brutally helpless about admitting, "I don't know what to say." If we are challenged in these dialogues with those closest to us, why would we volunteer that feeling for a stranger?

My capacity for Kind Communication will greatly limit (or expand) my ability to meet people's needs in all sorts of circumstances.

Kind Communication in Practice

Complimenting people (and developing the communication skills necessary to do so) is one of the most effective and low-burden exercises available for us to practice more Kindness in our lives. Unfortunately, the idea of the "compliment" has been reduced by our culture into a seemingly menial and confetti-like action. Generic gratitudes and platitudes have been co-opted by the greeting card industry and, as a by-product, Confetti Kindness gets printed and distributed at large.

Mass-produced Kindness is usually nonspecific and uninteresting.

Words matter. They are capable of inspiring masses and breaking hearts. They have an equal opportunity to hurt and to heal. We have to move beyond the widespread niceties that Kindness news stories or greeting cards can sometimes spread. Don't get me wrong, the clothespins that say, "You're Awesome!" or the cards that pun, "Con-grad-ulations!" are day-brighteners. But they usually aren't week-makers, month-changers, or lifesavers.

In its most raw and rewarding form, the skill of the "compliment" is the skill of seeing good in others and having the vocabulary and vulnerability to tell them about the good you see.

That's a skill we can all work on.

There is power in having a beautifully suited word or description for someone when they need it most. Thoughtfulness, paired with the vocabulary necessary to express that thoughtfulness, is a gifted combination that can create Deep Kindness that sticks.

Here are some of the most memorable compliments I've ever received:

- "When you speak, I see blue. Like the sky and like Kindness." —A high school girl with synesthesia in Texas

- "You talk about stuff that adults don't want to talk about. Thank you for being willing to be weird. It makes me feel like I'm not alone." —A middle school student in Washington

- "You're the kind of person I want to be around for your heart and want to learn from for your skill. That's a one-two punch and I can't get enough of being your friend." —My best friend

- "What you've taught me in my teaching has changed the way I've worked with kids for years. You've planted seeds that have shaped my life and the lives of so many students. It is impossible to know how far your influence goes." —An educator in Montana

- "You are a gifted performer with a servant's heart." —My mentor

When it comes to communicating Kindness, specificity is important. Think about the difference between receiving a Post-it Note with a generic compliment like "You're beautiful!" versus the handmade card or homemade phone call you receive that details how you've been influential in someone's life. One might give us a few moments of joy, while the other moves us profoundly. Why? Because Deep Kindness is generated from the hard work of building meaningful connections.

Kind Communication in Action

To give a genuine, powerful compliment you must first see something worthwhile in someone else, muster up the courage to say something, and then have the words to accurately articulate the goodness that you see.

Complimenting others can be fun, light, and playful, but it can also be an incredibly powerful exercise in celebrating and honoring people we care about. Specificity helps increase relevance to the recipient and makes it stick in their memory. Here are seven prompts to help put Kindness into action directed at specific people in your life. This exercise requires two parts: think of the first person who comes to mind that fits the description, then send a text or call to that person and fill in the blanks to practice some Kind Communication.

1. The person who is braver than anyone I know . . .
   "Superheroes have costumes, but you don't need a cape or mask to be _____. That time when you _____? Yeah, I remember thinking _____. Thank you for your bravery in this world."

2. The person who pushes me to believe in myself . . .
   "Without your constant _____ I would never have been able to accomplish _____. Because of you, I am _____ and _____, and I feel confident enough to do _____ in this world."

3. The person who enjoys dancing in the rain . . .
   "A free spirit like yours never minds getting _____. You are bold, _____, and _____. I am always inspired by your _____ and am forever grateful that we are _____."

4. The person who gives the best hugs . . .
   "Did you know that your hugs are _____? They make me feel like a _____ wrapped up in a _____. They are even better than _____."

5. The person who first introduced me to Kindness . . .
   "I am so grateful for your _____. Your Kindness has had a _____ effect on my life. I am _____ and _____ because of your influence."

6. The person who helps make the world a better place . . .
    "There is so much negativity in the world, but you have
    always been _____. I admire you so much for your
    _____ and am constantly inspired when I think of you
    doing _____. The world needs way more _____ and a whole
    lot more You."

7. The person who I share inside jokes with . . .
    "Remember that time when we _____? I will never forget
    how you _____ and I will always laugh when I think about
    _____."

These people each deserve their own kind of attention. Their own carefully
chosen words. Their own curated Kindness experience. They are more than
"pretty good," and our dexterity with language must catch up to the depth of
our love.

THE KIND OF KINDNESS THE WORLD NEEDS . . .

is specific and intentional. It is capable of identifying the unique
gifts that each person carries, and can express with rich clarity
why that quality is so important to the individual or to the world.
The kind of Kindness we need is one with a learned vocabulary
dedicated to healing wounds with attentive words and empow-
ering changemakers with thoughtful encouragements. It knows
that sometimes we are just a few inspiring words away from a
revelation or a revolution.

Chapter 9

EMOTIONAL REGULATION— CHOOSING HOW WE THINK

"Kids do well when they can."
—Dr. Ross Greene

My friend Annie, a brilliant child therapist, sent me this line from a book after we spent a weekend together building the curriculum for an annual summer leadership camp. It's a camp that has shaped both of our lives in some profound ways because of the paradigm shifts that are offered there. It's the first place I learned that you could *show love* to someone without even *liking them*. It was here that I came to understand that leadership was about your willingness to choose service over selfishness and compassion over convenience. Part of our weekend creating this year's curriculum was spent talking about the changing nature of the students who come through, and how the past fifteen years have changed kids in such a way that it begs our curriculum to adapt.

There is a natural hesitation to change something that you yourself have experienced as worthwhile. Many people come back to serve on a summer camp staff because they want others to have the same opportunity to be moved and changed in the ways that they were. But kids change, and sometimes that means our approach has to as well.

Annie and I spent time discussing this challenge, and how students today are showing up with more anxiety and mental health struggles than ever before. We noticed that students were more acutely aware of content that subtly reinforced old stereotypes around gender or race and they had no problem pushing back when they saw shortcomings. They had shorter attention spans, but longer perspectives.

Our discussion highlighted how hard it was for teachers to navigate this in the classroom. Most educators were taught to teach their subject areas, but few are taught to teach or respond to behavior. A lot of their work (and now ours, at this camp) has to do with navigating these behaviors more effectively in order to create a space for people to learn. Disruptive and dismissive behaviors make educating anyone, let alone a room full of thirty teenagers, quite onerous.

Annie said she wished that, instead of getting frustrated or angry, every teacher could instead look at students with this perspective: "Kids do well when they can."

This line from American clinical child psychologist Dr. Ross W. Greene suggests that, too often, we think kids "do well when they want to."[1] We often complain about a child's challenging behavior as a cry for attention, an exercise in laziness, or an attempt at manipulation. Greene believes that it's not a matter of desire, but a challenge of obstacle. It takes us back to the question, "What gets in the way?" and Greene's answer has two parts: lagging skills and unsolved problems.

Lagging skills would be the *why* of challenging behavior: if I am missing the social or emotional skills needed to address a situation (or if I don't have the language to navigate it successfully), my most natural reaction is to solve it with the tools at my disposal. And sometimes those tools look like anger, crying, or running away. You can think of lagging skills as internal factors that determine behavior. If the grocery store of my mind isn't stocked with a certain item, then my brain will either substitute it with a different, less desirable item or skip that ingredient altogether.

If lagging skills are the *why*, unsolved problems are the *who, what, when,* and *where* of challenging behavior. You can also think about them as external factors. When there are circumstances happening around me that cause me to feel overwhelmed, hurt, or confused, my emotional state is going to almost certainly drive some of my actions.

I would make one small change to Dr. Greene's proposal—replace "kids" with "people."

People do well when they can.

After all, there is no formal coming-of-age ceremony. There is no degree you get handed at a certain age, stating that your social and emotional skills are fully developed. And there is certainly no guarantee that, just because you're no longer a "kid," your unsolved problems are suddenly solved.

We all have lagging skills and unsolved problems. This undesirable duo is almost always at the root of any behavior we demonstrate that isn't fully in line with our ideal selves.

We all have stories of people in our lives who we thought were total jerks, only to find out that they were navigating some big or small tragedy in their life. Maybe they recently had a parent diagnosed with Alzheimer's and were spending all their limited spare time dealing with insurance paperwork and getting Mom set up in a fluorescent-lit facility. Perhaps they, for the third time, had a miscarriage after making it far enough in the pregnancy to decide on a name. Maybe you know someone in a marriage where their partner is charismatic and fun at all the parties, but quietly abusive when they get home.

And they don't know what to do about it.

Greene defines lagging skills as the by-product of the nearly invincible enemies of generational and educational shortcomings.[2] If you grow up in a family that doesn't have a skill like Emotional Regulation, you are not offered a role model of what that competency looks like. When schools do not teach Emotional Regulation as part of the curriculum, you find yourself in adulthood navigating challenges beyond your abilities.

To clarify, Emotional Regulation is "the ability to respond to the ongoing demands of experience with the range of emotions in a manner that is socially tolerable and sufficiently flexible to permit spontaneous reactions as well as the ability to delay spontaneous reactions as needed."[3]

Let's dive even deeper: "Emotional Regulation . . . involves initiating, inhibiting, or modulating one's state or behavior in a given situation—for example, the subjective experience (feelings), cognitive responses (thoughts), emotion-related physiological responses (heart rate or hormonal activity), and emotion-related behavior (bodily actions or expressions)."

To put it a bit more simply, there are a whole lot of skills required to be an effective, emotional human. And if you've been non-equipped or ill-equipped to handle certain situations where emotions come into play, you will almost certainly say or do things that aren't necessarily Kind to yourself or others.

Psychotherapy, neurobiology, developmental psychology, and many more fields are dedicated to the unpacking and understanding of our capacity to understand and regulate emotions. There are entire libraries dedicated to this stuff. We are emotional beings, and without key competencies, those emotions can control a substantial portion of our actions . . . even when we don't necessarily want them to.

I'll say it again: everyone *wants* to be Kind. But sometimes our desires don't match our abilities. If I have unsolved problems in my life (who doesn't?) and not enough tools in my toolbox to navigate them, there will be plenty of examples where my actions don't align with my ideals.

"People do well when they can" should be a humbling reminder that "can" is flexible and improvable. We have a moral imperative to teach and understand Emotional Regulation so our collective "can" can be better. For all of us adults who get to invent the curriculum for our life, we have a more personal imperative to reflect on our own skills and, using whatever tools we have now, see to it that we improve what we, ourselves, "can" do.

THE KIND OF KINDNESS THE WORLD NEEDS . . .

is one that is rooted in a deeply capable and thoughtfully cultivated emotional intelligence. When you can choose to be Kind regardless of how you feel, then your range of Kindness starts to expand to more than the people you already think like, act like, or just plain *like*. When your Kindness is no longer dependent on your fleeting feelings, you begin to develop a capacity for compassion that is more a function of discipline and less a function of drama.

Emotional Regulation in Action

Our personal emotional world is shaped by millions of inputs and is built upon a foundation of all kinds of experiences. We can easily feel overwhelmed by something that others may not because of some childhood hurt or trauma associated with that thing. One of my biggest emotional triggers is the feeling of being "dismissed." When I get ignored, physically or emotionally, my primal brain tries to take over and I want to lash out and demand attention. It's an auto-generated response that usually doesn't serve anyone in the situation positively.

Emotional Regulation grants us the gift of choice. Without it, you are beholden to your feelings; your decisions are based primarily on present circumstances and past traumas. But, as you develop your capacity for regulation, you offer yourself the freedom to make choices based on merit instead of anger. When you feel sad, you can choose to be Kind to the very person who made you sad. When you are feeling overwhelmed, you can choose to be Kind to yourself in a moment that could easily be self-destructive.

Here are a few ways that we can practice self-regulating:

Mindfulness

The skill of bringing active attention to the present. The state of observing thoughts and feelings without judging them as good or bad.

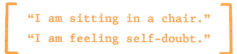

"I am sitting in a chair."
"I am feeling self-doubt."

It is a practice of bringing awareness to our physical and mental world while managing that inner critic that can sometimes be loud and value-twisting.

Try a two-part meditation today.

1. Find a seat at home or somewhere comfortable. Notice, without labeling or criticizing, the thoughts you are thinking.

See if you can be present to each thought for one to two minutes. At the end, write down three to five thoughts you had in the most neutral terms possible.

2. Take a five-minute walk and try to internally describe things without adjectives or labels. Instead of "pretty tree," try to objectively notice there is a tree. Perhaps you have never noticed this one before, but it is there, nonetheless. When you return home, write down three to five things you noticed in neutral terms.

These are exercises in non-attachment—a skill that, when cultivated, lays a solid foundation for healthy attachment. Oftentimes, our disappointment or resentment (or any other emotion that may drive us to be cruel instead of Kind) is born from unmet expectations. We develop thoughts around the way a thing is *supposed* to be to us—an attachment to the idea of how someone is *supposed* to behave or how a situation is *supposed* to play out. This is the kind of self-centered thinking that will lead us to perpetual frustration. Our expectations of what others are *supposed* to be is an attempt to deny that the only thing we really have any control over is ourselves.

Cognitive Reframing

According to Verywell Mind, cognitive reframing involves reinterpreting a situation in order to effectively adjust your emotional response to it.[4] When we are hurt by someone, we have a knack for twisting that hurtful action into a barbed wire that we think was crafted and swung specifically at *us*. Our naturally self-centered internal narrative wants to tell us that this person said or did that thing because they don't like us, or they think they are better than us. We concoct a story to best justify our anger or hurt. When we feel a painful feeling, we become our own prosecuting attorney so we can make a compelling case for why the other person did us wrong. Cognitive reframing is an exercise in selfless and generous imagination. It poses the question, "What if . . . ?" in a way that opens up the possibility that not everyone is out to get or hurt us.

"They didn't call me back; they hate me" becomes "They didn't call me back; they have been really overwhelmed and busy." Or, "She didn't invite me; I don't fit in" becomes "She wanted a really intimate group and I know she wants me at a future event."

Try writing out an example of an emotional reaction you had recently and the painful or unflattering story you told yourself. Then, write out a list of one to three other potential reinterpretations. Start with the most banal interpretation and advance to the most bizarre (just for fun) by the time you reach number three.

While maybe these new options are not probable, they are entirely possible. And isn't life suddenly much bigger (and much less self-centered) when you take the perspective of what is possible instead of making everything personal?

Emotional Vocabulary

How confidently would you say you know the difference between guilt and shame? Shame and embarrassment? Anger and disappointment? Aggravation and frustration? While some of it is semantics, it's a good reminder that all these distinctions have different results in your body and in the choices you might make as a result of them. Your clarity around these differences will help shape the way you handle them.

Try this exercise the next time you don't want to be Kind to someone. See how accurately you can label the feeling you assume they are feeling instead of the behavior they are displaying. Instead of thinking to yourself, "This person is being a jerk!" what if you tried, "This person must be feeling anguish or distress." Or, "They don't care for anyone but themselves" then becomes "They are feeling neglected and lonely."

This doesn't necessarily mean we will be correct in our assessments. But sometimes our ability to identify with someone's emotional state is easier than our ability to identify with their behavior. We tend to distance ourselves from behaviors that we find revolting, even though many of us are equally capable of the same actions. It is easier to relate to the *cause* of an ugly behavior than it is to claim familiarity with the behavior itself.

• • •

There will be plenty of people in your world that you don't *feel* like being Kind to because they frustrate you, annoy you, hurt you, or operate in ways that feel very different from your own behavior. But none of those things make them less deserving of Deep Kindness. Your capacity to identify and regulate your emotional state gives you the freedom of choice in moments that would otherwise be autopiloted by your feelings. With the hard-earned option you've granted yourself to *choose* despite the feelings of rage or hurt or jealousy, the only question that remains is: Are you willing to *choose* Kindness?

Chapter 10

EMPATHY—STANDING IN THE RAIN

*"Self-absorption in all its forms kills empathy, let alone compassion.
When we focus on ourselves, our world contracts as our
problems and preoccupations loom large. But when we focus on others,
our world expands. Our own problems drift to the periphery
of the mind and so seem smaller, and we increase our capacity for
connection—or compassionate action."*
—Daniel Goleman

In 2012 I traveled to Haiti to help out my incredible friends John and Merline, who run Haiti Partners—an organization that believes in helping Haitians change Haiti through education. They were welcoming their first class of three- and four-year-olds at the Children's Academy, a school they were building in Bawoysa—a poor and underserved area of the country. Their goal? Create a school that is the center of the community, supported by families and sustainable businesses, to serve as an epicenter for educational practices throughout Haiti.

Before 2012, I had never traveled to a country as challenged as Haiti. I stepped off the plane wearing some linen pants and a fedora and was quickly met by the contrast of this place—joy and tragedy so often sit side by side. The people were dancing, smiling, and so dang friendly. There was color and life amid the backdrop of broken concrete and pain. The evidence of their massive earthquake was still intensely raw. Driving through Port-au-Prince painted a picture of poverty that I'd never had to wrestle with so intimately. The gift of seeing news like Haiti's through a screen is that we can fade to black whenever it gets too uncomfortable. But here it was in full color: animals and children foraging for food in a sea of garbage. Shantytowns that house hundreds side by side by side by side.

We drove an hour to John and Merline's home. Stepping out of the car, we were greeted by the loveliest serenade: twenty kids singing words I didn't understand, but it didn't matter—hope and beauty are always translatable.

Haiti Partners has all kinds of tremendous projects to help support this community. One of their groups is called WOZO, a children's choir comprised of kids ages five through eighteen. In Haitian Creole, *wozo* means "bamboo reed." The choir's motto is, "We bend but we do not break."

Resilience is a natural and abundant resource here.

John and Merline's own kids were five and nine at the time. They came running outside and you could tell they were so excited about what they kept calling "the Big Event." In just a few days' time, WOZO was performing a big concert as part of a series of performances hosted by the brand Life Is Good. The concert was to be in the big city at a big park and it was a BIG deal.

Saturday rolled around—the day of "the Big Event"—and WOZO showed up ready to be rock stars. It was over a hundred degrees outside and the humidity could have drowned you standing up. The bus arrived three hours late. The group, as you can imagine, was well cooked.

To call it a bus, I should tell you, is an overstatement. It was really more of a twelve-passenger van, and all twenty-plus students piled in, with no AC, on a day that would melt most people's brains. They traveled over an hour, down winding roads into the city.

Upon arrival, the members of WOZO were informed that the event was behind schedule and their set had to be cut down a bit. Still, they enthusiastically got into their performance outfits, got onstage, and sang their hearts out. I had no idea what they were saying, but it didn't matter—passion and persistence are always translatable.

As they filed offstage and the day wrapped up, a massive thunderstorm rolled in from the distance. The kids piled back into the van, but we realized we were able to take six students ourselves in the back of our SUV. Right as they climbed inside, the rain was on top of us.

Rain in Haiti is not a gentle experience—it's like an ocean has been inverted and she's trying to find her way back to land. The streets quickly started to flood, and we plowed our way through, for over an hour, back toward Bawoysa. The rain was relentless and the thunder felt like it was inside the seats. After a particularly loud boom, one of the five-year-old girls in the back started crying. I wanted so badly to say something, but I didn't speak their language.

I didn't need to. As I turned in my seat, the other girls all grabbed the smallest girl's hand and they started to sing to her. I had no idea what they were saying, but it didn't matter—comfort and compassion are always translatable.

Finally, we arrived at our first stop. John hopped out of the car, opened the back, and helped one of the girls out. A brother was waiting, in the pouring rain, for his sister. They all hugged, John got back in the car, and we headed to another stop. I learned that some of these girls would have to walk two miles to get to their homes beyond passable roads.

We stopped five more times and, each time, John got out of the car, helped a girl out, and walked her to her family—always greeting them, hugging them, and making sure the girls headed out safely.

Finally, it was just our small group in the car. John was drenched head to toe and back again.

I wanted to comfort him, so I placed my hand on his shoulder: "I'm so sorry, John."

His brother, Jesse, chimed in with some levity: "If something like this happened in the States, there would be lawsuits! We aren't as tough as we'd like to pretend back home."

I wanted to console John: "I know today was the Big Event and it seems like everything that could have gone wrong, did. And look at you! You are soaked. Everything is soaked."

John turned around in his seat. He smiled big, water dripping from his eyelashes.

"Houston, this was the best day of many of these kids' lives. I saw their smiles and felt their pride when they hugged me goodbye. And the rain? If they'd let me, I would stand in the rain all night with them."

Sometimes lessons in Kindness sneak up on you. They can hit you like a wet SUV.

For a long time, I thought empathy was a complicated thing that required you to have lived through a lot of pain before you were able to empathize with someone else's. But I realized on that damp night that we all have three rather profound, everyday choices about how we engage with the world around us:

APATHY: I don't care if others get wet if I get to stay dry.
SYMPATHY: Here's an umbrella, hope it helps.
EMPATHY: Standing in the rain, together.

I will never know the full scope of suffering that many of the people of Haiti have endured. I haven't suffered through huge natural disasters. I haven't lived on just a dollar or two a day. I haven't worn hand-me-downs of hand-me-downs. I haven't known the pain of losing a loved one to a simple, treatable virus. I haven't walked miles for my education or for my water. But I suppose I do know what it feels like to be soaking wet. And perhaps, even just for a moment, that can be enough. To be there with another person and be present to their pain, even if you can't identify with the precise story of it. To not run from the hurt or try to solve the problem, but to sit with it. To listen to it. To embrace it. That's empathy.

Victor Frankl, the Holocaust survivor who wrote *Man's Search for Meaning*, describes suffering like a gas. He says gas, like hurt, expands to fill whatever container it is in. Meaning that while, objectively, a middle schooler navigating their parents' divorce may seem to be in less pain than the twelve-year-old Haitian who just lost her mom to the flu, the emotional suffering inside the body actually feels very similar physiologically. We only know what we know, so our individual perspective shapes our personal experience with pain. The worst suffering in my world to me actually feels quite similar to the worst suffering in your world for you.

That is one version of what Kindness is—standing in the rain. To be willing to sacrifice not just your time or your money, but your comfort, your pride, your fearfulness—your dryness—in order to truly *be alongside* another person. *With* someone.

The Big Event had nothing to do with the concert in the park. The Big Event was those girls, singing in the back of the car, and hugging John in the rain.

Empathy in Practice

Empathy is the most in-demand skill in our workforce today. It makes sense: organizations can compile data and systemize actions, but their ability to understand that data and tap into what people want, need, and *feel* is priceless in a world becoming progressively more automated.

My friend Barbara Gruener, a longtime counselor and general superhero, says that empathy gives Kindness its *why*. When I understand someone deeply, when I begin to truly feel *with* them, I have a clear sense of their hurt and their need. The most powerful Kindness is the one that meets and treats a deep need. Not the airport massage chair that barely touches the whole body—we are talking about the deep-tissue massage from an intuitive and thoughtful healer who has asked where you need the most attention and approaches the area with skilled and sensitive hands.

Just like Kindness has different types of impact (Common Kindness, Confetti Kindness, and Deep Kindness), empathy has different levels of effectiveness. Not all empathy is created equal. We can sometimes find ourselves moving on the periphery of someone else's perspective. This is what I call Shallow Empathy. Acts of Shallow Empathy are still important, but they do not always leave a deep impact on the people we are trying to help.

The Sandy Hook tragedy provides some great examples of Shallow Empathy—of well-intentioned, but non-empathetic, Kindness. In the aftermath of the shooting, the school was sent tens of thousands of teddy bears. Just weeks after the event, the town had to rent a twenty-thousand-square-foot warehouse to hold them all. At the candlelit vigil, stuffed animals outnumbered attendees.

Matt Cole, one of the vigil organizers, provides a chastening perspective: "A teddy bear is wonderful, but a teddy bear can't pay for counseling. A teddy bear can't pay for a funeral."[1]

On the far side of the empathy spectrum, we can find ourselves soul-merging with another person when we become more open, attuned, and skilled. This is Deep Empathy. John's willingness to stand in the rain all night with the WOZO choir to see them to safety and to be with them in their pride, joy, and fear—that is Deep Empathy in action.

Deep Empathy allows us to discover and unpack *need*. This very personal and closely held thing that all of us have, but no two versions of it look alike. When we seek to understand and fully examine this thing in others over time, we can practice Kindness in ways that are deeply healing instead of shallowly helpful.

It is a humbling reminder that while we might be doing something that could be called an "act of Kindness," we actually may not be helping. We may be doing a thing that *we* believe is worthwhile, but it doesn't guarantee the receiving party even wants that thing. Listening and understanding are the foundation upon which we build thoughtful generosity. When we deeply know *why* someone needs a certain type of Kindness, the action becomes so much more thoughtful, specific, and purposeful. Deep Empathy and Kindness meet people where they are and make an impact that is personal and profound.

THE KIND OF KINDNESS THE WORLD NEEDS . . .

is one that pays better attention. It listens well in order to love better.

Empathy in Action

In the toolbox of empathy, it helps to have strong listening skills. I'd put Emotional Awareness and Perspective-Taking in there, too. My hope for this book is to not only illuminate areas of potential growth but provide a bit of a workout plan to get there.

Picture wading into the ocean. At first you are just standing and getting splashed by the waves (Shallow Empathy). This requires less overall effort but is still a valuable and palpable experience. The next level is where you wade in and start to swim. You can still touch bottom if you need to, but your body has had to adjust to some new temperatures, and you've gotten your hair wet. Maybe even touched seaweed. Finally, you strap on an oxygen tank and dive deep! You are choosing to adapt yourself to an environment that is fully unfamiliar, and there are definitive risks involved like equipment failure or creepy crawlies. This is Deep Empathy.

It's usually easier to empathize with people with who we feel inherent overlap. People who have lived similar lives or hold similar beliefs are more easily accessible for our brains. We can quickly identify with and understand them. So, for the sake of a better workout, let's focus on exercising empathy with people who are, in some way, distinctly *different*. Here are a few empathetic exercises to try with varying levels of "depth."

Practicing empathy is just like swimming—the deeper you go when practicing, the more you may feel uncomfortable or underprepared. So offer yourself some patience and work your way slowly into the "deep end."

Practicing empathy with someone from . . .

1. A DIFFERENT CULTURE

STANDING: Ask someone to share, if they are willing, about their favorite tradition in their culture. Don't interrupt with your own stories; instead, ask follow-up questions about their answer.

SWIMMING: Invite someone to have a cross-cultural cuisine night. Share your favorite dish and ask them to prepare theirs. Discuss what it is about the dish that makes it a favorite. Bonus points if you work to make the meal together!

SCUBA DIVING: Attend a cultural event with someone. Before you go, ask them to explain some of the routines or rituals that make it special and learn the history of that event. If the person doesn't know the history, research it together! If appropriate, participate as much as possible.

2. A DIFFERENT RACE

STANDING: Talk with someone who is a different race than you about what Kindness has meant to them in their life. What is a moment of Kindness that is important to them? Who are their Kindness role models? What is an act of Kindness they are proud of? After your conversation, see if you can reflect on one or two ways you

- think about Kindness differently and one or two ways that you think about Kindness the same.
- **SWIMMING:** Learn three facts about the racial history of a race different from yours. If it helps, use these guiding questions: 1) What is an event or time period that improved the lives of many people from this race? Why and how? 2) What is an event or time period that worsened the lives of many people from this race? Why and how? 3) Compare and contrast the struggles/successes you think someone from this race experienced one generation ago. Two? Three?

SCUBA DIVING: Ongoing racial disparity is often a result of broken systems. One of the most important systems that has sprawling impact is education. Identify a race that you know has historically experienced oppression and spend time learning deeply (in such a way that you could explain meaningful details to a friend or family member) about how educational systems support and don't support people of this race effectively. Commit to one meaningful action (voting, local engagement, fundraising) that can help to close these gaps.

3. A DIFFERENT COUNTRY

STANDING: Ask someone from another country what a typical day is like where they are from. What are the kinds of foods they eat? What is family life like? What are the stores or activities like there? What are the customs that exist that they've noticed don't exist here? If you don't know anyone directly, see if you can find someone who has parents or grandparents who have emigrated and ask them!

SWIMMING: Commit to learning the ten most common and useful words or phrases in a language different from your own. Try to practice with someone who speaks the language fluently or do some online video tutorial watching. Bonus points if you learn translations for words related to emotions so you can better talk empathetically in that language.

SCUBA DIVING: Go on an excursion through your city or a nearby city with a person who didn't grow up in your country. Try to find some activities that give you an opportunity to share something local, while they reflect on what it is like back home. Maybe go to an art museum, a restaurant, or a market, or go see a documentary. If you can't find anything in person, do some internet scouring together to learn about the history of their products, art, or food.

4. A DIFFERENT IDENTITY (GENDER IDENTITY, SEXUAL ORIENTATION)

STANDING: *"I believe gender is a spectrum, and I fall somewhere between Channing Tatum and Winnie the Pooh."* —Stephen Colbert. Identify, for fun, what two people or things you are "between" and ask a friend to do the same about themselves. Use this to start a conversation about gender, identity, and how you two might differ or overlap.

SWIMMING: Ask someone older than you who you trust (parents, guardians, mentors) how they came to their current understanding of gender and/or sexuality, and reflect on the ways in which you align with them or are different from them and why.

SCUBA DIVING: Watch or read a piece written by someone who has a different sexual identity, gender identity, or orientation than you. Seek out videos or articles that detail a story of how they came to understand their identity and what struggles they have faced along the way. If possible, process this with someone who identifies in a similar way.

5. A DIFFERENT SET OF BELIEFS

STANDING: Ask someone with different beliefs from you what they love most about their belief system and why. If they are willing, give them space to share the story of how they came to their beliefs and any struggles or doubts they've experienced along the way.

SWIMMING: Offer an "Ideology Exchange" with a friend. Write down your top five most important things or ideas about your belief system and have them do the same. Then, find a piece of writing that you feel most exemplifies or solidifies your beliefs (and have them do the same). Sit down and share the lists and readings with each other and talk about what you noticed in common and, without judgment, what was different.

○ **SCUBA DIVING:** Commit to a "Belief Buffet." Choose three religions, belief systems, or places of worship that you'd like to learn more about and, if you are able, go participate in their ceremonies, rituals, or services for at least one session. Be up-front with those in charge about what you are doing and ask if you can be a guest in their space to learn more through experience! When you've sampled some new spiritual options, spend some time reflecting on what you appreciated about each.

Chapter 11

VULNERABILITY—THE COURAGE TO CARE

"The best people possess a feeling for beauty, the courage to take risks, the discipline to tell the truth, the capacity for sacrifice. Ironically, their virtues make them vulnerable; they are often wounded, sometimes destroyed."
—*Ernest Hemingway*

Sometimes I worry that I've made myself into a robot. The amount of time I spend thinking about other people's emotional intelligence has, in some ways, caused the death of my own. Overintellectualizing something that is, by design, emotional sets the stage for a weird dissonance between understanding and feeling.

I know what I'm *supposed* to feel, but I can't always get there.

During the busiest years of my speaking career, the robotic armor I'd constructed for myself was a slow cooker recipe of travel, repetition, and lots of listening "from a distance." Wandering around to six hundred schools over the course of seven years makes for a specific kind of exhaustion involving upright plane naps and time-zone hopscotching. Speaking in five states in five days is daunting logistically. Saying the same thing in each place, repeatedly, feels internally torturous.

Don't get me wrong, I believe fully in what I've shared in schools and feel deep gratitude for the platforms I have been given to tell meaningful stories. The part I couldn't have predicted is how bored I'd get of *myself*. I couldn't have guessed at how trapped I'd start to feel between expertise and expansion: people were paying me to deliver a speech that I'd given hundreds of times, which left seemingly little room for creative exploration. You better deliver your best stuff—the stuff you know works—when there are eighteen hundred high school kids in a crowded gymnasium and the school administrators paid to fly you cross-country from Washington. Or Iowa. Or Florida. Or wherever I was the night before.

So, I continued to deliver. And the better I got at giving this talk, the more I found students coming up to me afterward, wanting to share how my story affected theirs. This is a phenomenon I refer to as the "Safety of the Stranger." As a guest in the building who is only there for a day and has willingly shared all my stories, I am a ripe target for people to share all of their darkest and ugliest challenges. I have no connection to any of their friends or family, so I seem like a reasonable passing cargo ship for them to offload some of their pain.

I listened. Each beautiful soul had a story to share and some of them, at age thirteen, had lived through more suffering than anyone deserves in a lifetime. I've heard stories of abuse, of suicidal ideation or attempts, of coming out to receptive parents, of coming out to non-receptive parents, of breakups and breakdowns, and of the quieter suffering of feeling deeply alone, weird, or unseen.

I'm not a trained therapist, so I've made it my mission to just listen. To receive these students and let them know that someone is attuned to their hearts and that someone cares. I point them toward other adults or people in their lives that can support their ongoing healing. I give them a hug and let them know they are loved. I offer hope without giving advice.

But even in my distant role as a transient friend and not a certified counselor, I can't avoid letting some of the stories stick. I'd hop in my rental car to head back to some regional airport with the residue of suffering in my carry-on. The next morning, I'd depart from a new Hampton Inn, in a new rental car, to a new school, to hear new stories that may just break your heart.

Over the years, you start to steel yourself against the exhaustion, the repetition, and the listening. You listen to these young people's stories, but you don't take them on personally; you chew, but you don't swallow. You just don't have the emotional room for it all.

And slowly and subconsciously, you arrive at . . . RoboSpeaker.

Imagine the picture of positivity wandering from school to school telling stories of love and Kindness. My message was about our ability to choose our actions despite our feelings, and I was saying it with such repetitive gumption that I had acted my way out of my own emotionality. In sharing so repeatedly about the vulnerability of Kindness, I'd made myself invulnerable.

And so I was forever "fine." Or, more commonly, "Great!"

We are all a bit addicted to saying, "I'm fine." You play the part for long enough, and it starts to feel familiar on the tongue.

When I say the words, "How are you?" I bet there is some level of automatic programming that kicks in just dying to say, "I'm fine; how are you?" We do it all the time and it's actually a weirdly deadening answer to a potentially vibrant question. We find ourselves in these prisons of pleasantries all the time, even though we are all craving more authentic, vulnerable answers.

My friend Esteban likes to say that we are all just two "How are you?"s away from a breakdown.

"How are you?"

"Fine!"

"No, *how are you?*"

Weeping. Thrashing. Tantrums. A full breakdown into a pile of long-held-up mush.

We think that this sort of emotional fire hydrant–ing is what vulnerability looks like—if you keep emotions pent up for long enough, the dam-breaking will almost always feel cathartic. But flooding plants with buckets of water is hardly a replacement for consistent care.

So, often we wait until we are desperate for a connection before we seek it. Experiencing the sharp contrast, then, between "totally fine" and "falling apart" deceives us into thinking we are making progress. That's not vulnerability; it's victimhood. In our false perception that vulnerability is a public unraveling, we sometimes find comfort in the aid that rushes in when we claim the need for triage.

In our culture's broad-sweeping emotional illiteracy, we have this belief that if we cry, then we've had a powerful experience. But crying isn't always a sign of vulnerability. We can be moved or manipulated into an emotional experience, but that doesn't guarantee that we are actually experiencing connection, understanding, or the potential for real growth. Breakdowns do not always equate to breakthroughs.

There is a delicate balance to vulnerability that often swings between two states: keep-it-all-together stoicism or full-blown, tear-tsunamic oversharing. There is a competency to this balancing act that, if not exercised, actually reduces our capacity for Kindness.

You see, while crying may not always be vulnerable, *caring* is.

A few years back, I was speaking at a high school in Washington. The occasion was in honor of Martin Luther King Jr., and I was giving a talk about love. The premise of the talk is that, while we will forget about 99 percent of our life, the little actions of love we give others could live in the 1 percent that people never forget. It is intended as a powerful reminder that our daily forgettable moments are potentially unforgettable to someone else. Love, and the actions associated with it, is like any other muscle in our body and should be worked out with regularity in order to maximize this potential impact.

I was getting to the climax of the talk where I try to offer a paradigm shift to high schoolers about the difference between love as a *feeling* and love as a *choice*. Off to my right side, about halfway up the bleachers, some male upperclassman yelled out, "Who cares?"

I went through a little mental checklist to see whether or not I should acknowledge the comment or just move on. Sometimes moments like this are better left totally ignored. But there were too many eyes now curious about how I might respond, so in we go.

"Who cares?!" I began.

"Perhaps that is exactly the problem. Not *enough* people care. And as a result, over the course of history, we've let really awful things happen to a whole lot of people. Who *cared* about ending slavery or segregation? Who *cared* about the genocide in Rwanda or in Germany? Who *cares* about the increase of teenage suicide or rampant school shootings? In the absence of enough people caring, we are capable of selfish and terrible things in this world."

Conversations like this tap into a deep well of frustration and passion for me. I barely took a breath.

"The problem is that we've convinced each other that it's *cool not to care.* Apathy is a successful marketing campaign created by the scared and the small; the people who have stepped back from action usually do so because they've failed once or twice at stepping up. So let's not kid ourselves: it's not cool not to care, it's just *easier* not to care.

"When you care," I went on, "you expose yourself to risk: the risk that you may get laughed at or judged or mocked. You risk failure or feeling rejected. And each time something like that happens, the fear part of our brain— the part that is primal and self-preservational—tries to protect us. It says, 'Don't do that again!' because it doesn't want you to feel humiliated, helpless, judged, or incapable. The bravest among us have that same voice in their brain; they just choose to ignore it. They choose against fear and toward action. They choose love, even when that choice is wildly inconvenient or uncomfortable or it doesn't serve them.

"The act of caring is terrifying and that's what makes it vulnerable. There is a frustratingly direct relationship between Kindness and vulnerability: the more I care, the more likely I am to get hurt. And so we collectively put our tails between our legs and try to pretend that an apathetic life is anything but the smallest, most selfish way to live.

"Who *cares*?! Not enough of us. But those that do will do it despite the potential pain, because they know that the world deserves better than what we have today. They know that they are just as obligated as anyone else to lay their reputation and ego on the line to step up and participate in making this world a more Kind and caring place.

"Dr. Martin Luther King Jr. wasn't born as a prince with power or elected into a position of leadership. He chose to walk into the fire—to put his life on the line—because he knew that caring was the only pathway to a more just world. He was fully aware that it was a pathway that was overgrown and filled with all sorts of thorns and traps, but he walked it anyway. So, who cares? Well, perhaps you should. Perhaps we all should."

The disrupter didn't say anything for the rest of the assembly.

I got a message from him five years later with an apology and a short note: "Hey, Houston. I'm sorry for what I said that day. I was angry and there was a lot going on in my life. I look at what you do now and I respect it a lot! It's really hard to care (I'm learning this all the time), but it makes a difference. You make a difference. And I know I can, too. High-school me just didn't yet understand."

Simple, small notes in the spam folder of my Facebook inbox are an example of the Big Events of this job. I treasure notes like this where, years later, something clicks, and suddenly my seemingly silly stories become seriously relevant for someone when they need them. These kinds of notes move me into greater action and propel my heart forward in this work.

Maybe I'm not a robot after all.

Vulnerability lives in all of us in different shapes and sizes. But, when it comes to a Kinder world, the kind of Kindness I'm talking about isn't robotic pleasantries. Neither is it the emotional fire hydrant–ing of our traumas revealed publicly for all to witness. To care is to choose to dream of a better world and actually do something to create it. Something that we can't (yet) program any robot to do.

THE KIND OF KINDNESS THE WORLD NEEDS . . .

is the vulnerable understanding that Kindness will almost always cost us our comfort and usually our convenience. The nature of caring involves exposing your neck (and your reputation) to the teeth of culture and to those people too fearful to be bigger than their insecurities. It's tough to publicly cry, but it's tougher to publicly care.

Vulnerability in Action

The act of caring is not a passive thing. If we don't align our actions to what we say we care about, we are creating an ideal imaginary world, not a real one. Meaningful dreams might feel ambitious, but the choice to make them happen is vulnerable.

Here are a few categories of caring that will help you focus your practical pursuit. Over the next week, see if you can find an opportunity to get some vulnerability reps in for each person or people.

- **YOURSELF:** Practice dressing different today as a small exercise in vulnerability. Try overdressing or underdressing (or being expressive in your dressing) for the day. Own it and experience standing *out* in this small way so you can work toward standing *up* for something bigger.

- **FAMILY:** Call someone in your family and ask them to help you navigate a challenge you are having in your life right now. Ask them questions about their own experience with a similar issue (try to call someone who you know has worked through a related experience).

- **FRIEND:** Ask your friend for three specific things that you could do to be a better friend. Open up an honest dialogue about what these gaps are and how you can close them.

- **COMMUNITY:** Go to a new place in your area in which you've never really spent time. By yourself. Without your phone on you or out in front of you. See if you can meet one new person who is outside your normal group, even just to learn their name.

- **WORLD:** Identify one cause that you believe in. Spend an hour doing some deeper research than usual on this cause. Write something somewhere (digitally, probably) that can be seen publicly about this cause and why you want to help in this area.

To boldly care about yourself, your friends, your family, your community, and your world means that you will likely find yourself, on many occasions, standing alone while facing criticism, animosity, doubters, and downright failures. Remember, it's easier to laugh at the person caring than it is to *be* the person caring. Everyday vulnerability requires us to maintain a disposition toward courage. Active caring almost always risks something meaningful to us.

Deep Kindness asks us to dream so vividly big that the risks feel manageable when compared to the good that is possible on the other side of our action.

With Deep Kindness, there are risks. As the next chapter outlines, big dreams can come at unexpected costs. When it is time to count those costs, other skills are required to navigate those hurdles with Kindness.

Chapter 12

FORGIVENESS—
PEOPLE AND THEIR BEHAVIORS

"Each of us is more than the worst thing we've ever done."
—Bryan Stevenson

And so I held her, shaking. It was our final hug and it felt like failure; I was losing my wife because I had lost her heart.

It was a seven-year relationship and much of the whole thing was a grand adventure. After two years of relentless companionship, we got engaged on a mountaintop. The internet shared the video of that precious moment. The content was quintessential, commentable romance. A year later, we got married in the forest. We danced under a full moon with 250 friends and family. Three years later, I was holding the woman I'd loved in my arms while she grieved love that no longer lived.

Rewind, for a moment, to a week before our wedding in 2014. I gave a speech in Orlando that had a profound impact on my speaking career. It was a national conference for student leaders and I was doing a "showcase" in an attempt to be hired by teachers and statewide conference coordinators.

It went better than I could have dared to dream.

After that talk in Orlando, I started getting booked more frequently for events all over the country. Texas Association of Student Councils. The South Carolina State Leadership Conference. New York. New Mexico. Oklahoma. I was busier than ever and increasingly distant from home. And home is where my wife's heart was.

The success of the week before my marriage would ultimately shape the end of it.

Being away from home was challenging for more than just its physical departures. Working relentlessly in schools talking about Kindness keeps you very accountable for seeming "Kind," always. The world had pitched a particular aesthetic of Kindness to me: full-scale smiles, endless enthusiasm, and a bubbly way of being that, over time, began a sort of death to any deep relationship I had with myself (see previous chapter).

I often felt reduced into one-dimensionality. I spent so much time setting and resetting the charming face and the nice-to-meet-you attitude that I *became* a First Impression.

I would travel to two or sometimes three schools a day to deliver a talk on Kindness and, each time, I would start from scratch in a relational sense. Always the same message, just delivered to all new faces. It's a necessity in my work to rapidly develop a level of trust with an audience that might make me worthy, in their eyes, of accepting or feeling moved by my stories. Over time, I got really effective at One-Day Relationships.

One-Day Relationships are great for an audience, but they're the opposite for intimacy.

I would pour my heart and energy into every school and audience I encountered, travel home via Hot Dog Seats and Hampton Inn layovers, and finally be there. Exhausted. With just enough time to do some laundry and repack for the next trip.

There was no energy left for myself, let alone for my partner. All those short-term relationships left me feeling sadly shallow in my long-term one. I didn't know how to move past the First Impression version of myself, even in my personal life. Over time, like a remodeled old house, I no longer recognized my original design. I was emotionally walled off and my sense of self was scattered and shallow. I talked and thought exclusively about work and slowly arranged the entirety of our shared life to serve my personal narrative. There was sparse space in the calendar for quality time, and meaningful conversation was beholden to my convenience.

If not handled thoughtfully, your professional passions can consume your personal priorities. And the more noble we self-perceive our cause to be, the more we can self-justify the relentless work.

I was more married to my purpose than to my partner—a dynamic that is sustainable in sprints, but not well-suited for marathons.

Don't get me wrong, we had a lot of amazing times and my wife was an incredible life partner and travel buddy. We adventured the heck out of the world and got to do some epic, silly, and wonderful things together.

But the highest peaks will never be grand enough to combat the persistent and wide valleys.

There was just too much time away, too few tools in our toolbox, and not enough role models for us to lean on. My ongoing need to be surrounded and successful left her feeling alone and abandoned. And even after she shared thoughtful, repeated requests for me to slow down, I didn't.

I could tell I was losing her. She became increasingly resentful and conflicts that should have been matches felt more like bonfires. The busier I got, the more exhausted I would show up to any attempts at healing. I felt like a fatigued doctor doing heart-opening surgery and I refused to admit how reckless that was or that I was in control of my own rest. Instead, I masked insecurity and being overwhelmed with anger and blame.

One night, she quietly asked for my attention and I responded by shouting at her for buying a bathing suit. How dare she want to relax at the beach, I thought, when I was working so hard from the road? The audiences appreciated me, so why couldn't she? These are the sorts of self-indignant internal dialogues that build resentment while they erode connection.

Kicking and screaming, I refused to let myself admit my deepest fear: in a career built on teaching selflessness, I had become a deeply selfish husband. I talked about love for a living and couldn't figure out how to show up for the love of my life.

We tried like crazy for a year. Retreats, workbooks, and counseling. Couples therapy and individual sessions. I sat in the "sad chair" during therapy many times with a Kind woman who tried to help me feel more than one dimension. Occasionally, we would find some breakthroughs and there would be momentary relief and normalcy. We'd temporarily stop the bleeding, but the wounds weren't as external as we'd hoped. And I just don't think we knew how to navigate all the symptoms.

We finally arrived at a tipping point. My speaking mentor also happens to be a marriage and family therapist. We went to him in a final attempt at help, and he was a brilliant mirror for our hurt and struggle. After six hours of heart-wrenching triage, his ultimate recommendation was that we take time apart to work on ourselves. The intention, if we were lucky, would be that our individual paths toward health and healing would meet back into a shared one.

The only rule of the six-week break was that we had to commit to our own personal work—to give our best shot at our own growth with the possibility of saving our marriage.

We sat in a weighted silence on the drive home, each of us contemplating the unmapped emotional space ahead of us. By the time we got home, my wife was weeping. The tears were profound, seemingly endless, and came from a sadness that felt entirely unique.

In a sudden, tragic moment, I knew she was done. Done trying. Done with us. I think it was occurring to her all at once, too. She'd already given it her very best shot and I'd proven her worst fears right too many times. While perhaps I felt like this was a fresh attempt, she knew it was just a fresh coat of paint on a wall that had internal rot. She was living in a heart beyond hope and I knew, with brutal clarity, that we were beyond repair.

And so I held her, shaking, while we grieved a chance we'd never get. It was a final hug and it felt like failure.

We lingered there in a moment of shared finality and time unhinged. We grieved the children we wouldn't have and the weddings we wouldn't attend. We wept over the unplanned trips that would never get booked. The pets that we'd never name. The recipes that we'd never cook together.

We grieved a lifetime of love that would never be lived. The weight of it felt unbearable and the haunting voice of shame kept repeating: "If only you'd listened a little earlier."

A few weeks later, we sat together on the couch. It used to be "our couch" but, under new circumstances, it felt more like a showroom model. We held hands in a way that was both familiar and foreign while we came to a hard conclusion: the Kindest thing we knew how to do—the best way we knew how to love each other—was to divorce each other.

It didn't take long for anger to arrive. All the therapy-born, slow-nurtured seedlings of personal insight were replaced with the fast-growing weeds of rage. "I should have listened to her sooner" turned quickly to "Nothing was good enough for her, anyway." "I wasn't emotionally available" became "She needed too much attention."

When we are emotionally unhealthy and find ourselves humbled, we turn off the potential for wisdom in favor of weapons. It's easier to lash out than it is to simply listen.

I stayed angry at her for a long time because I felt like she didn't give that final attempt a proper shot. We had a clear plan and someone to walk us through it. It seemed like she was walking away right when I was showing up. I was finally ready to run the race and didn't want to acknowledge that I was arriving long after everyone had packed up.

It started as a distant thunderclap—a rumbling that foretold future pain that hadn't yet arrived. I was able to protect myself from the despair of shame by focusing on blame. The "how dare she"s and "why didn't she"s were a distracting refrain that I played over the top of a much more terrifying backing track. And then one night, it all fell apart. The backing track became a deafening melody: *I* wasn't enough. I failed her. I was more married to my mission than I was to my wife.

I was angry at her because she gave up on our marriage. I was ashamed of myself because I had given up first.

When the realization struck, I ended up curled around my toilet, vomiting. Crawling into my bed, my heart was racing and I thought I was having a heart attack. My sheets were sweaty and I had 911 pulled up on my phone. I called my dad instead. He happened to be visiting from out of town and was staying at a nearby hotel. In the most tender moment I can remember with my father, he drove over, lay in bed next to me, and quietly held my hand. Up until that point, I hadn't told him anything about the unraveling of my marriage. Nothing. I was terrified to admit that I couldn't manage it all on my own, and angry at myself that I might have been the cause.

My dad lay there and listened to me that night and passed no judgment. In this rare occurrence, he offered no opinion. But I had one: I lost my wife because I lost her heart. I messed up and all I could feel was rage or shame or some combination of the two.

I was in deep pain and in need of an opposing force; Kindness's most understated partner is forgiveness.

Forgiveness, I learned through trial and fire, is separating the person from the behavior.

We do bad things; we are not bad people.

The story of our marriage was one of many forgivings. At the climax of pain, we were able to hold each other close and recognize that our behaviors were the by-product of a lot of hurt and confusion, and being ill-equipped to handle it all. There should be a holiday around this concept—we need as many Forgivings as we do Thanksgivings.

I've had to continually work on forgiving her and myself for the challenging mess we arrived at. In the time that has passed, I've separated the person (her) from the behavior ("giving up on our marriage"), and that distance has allowed me to take ownership over the role I played in this whole story. When I was able to take ten steps back, I saw clearly how I hadn't made her my priority and then I blamed *her* for her hurt. So, I've also had to separate the person (me) from the behavior (avoidance, selfishness) and unpack the ways that I ran from intimacy and why.

Over time, she has given me the gift of forgiveness, too. I'm grateful for the friendship and healing we've navigated, together. Every few months, we will catch up about things both meaningful and mundane and there is a comforting compassion that holds the conversation together. We usually sit on the couch.

Forgiveness is about seeing the space in between the human and the hurt. There is a reason for *every* behavior and, if we can handle the inquiry into that reason with care and Kindness, we can manage to release ourselves and others from a lot of pain.

Did you know that forgiveness is closely associated with happiness? There are all kinds of data points, both analytical and anecdotal, that remind us that resentment is a surefire pathway to misery. To hold on to anger toward yourself or others is like putting your hand on a hot stove—you feel alive, but you look dumb. The longer you hold it there, the more likely the damage will be permanent.

Separating the person from their behavior doesn't justify the behavior. We can and should hold people accountable when they do things that hurt us, and draw clear boundaries that say, "This is not okay. You won't do this to me again."

Forgiveness just means that we do not take pain as personally. It gives us freedom from a terrible fear: that we actually deserved the damage we were dealt. The Kindest thing you can do for *yourself* is to forgive those people who've hurt you the most. Along the way, you may discover that you're high on that list.

THE KIND OF KINDNESS THE WORLD NEEDS . . .

is the sort that separates people from their pain and acknowledges that our worst behaviors are more often by-products of suffering than intentional decisions of disdain. Deep Kindness requires us to see past the barbs thrown our way to note that most outward spikes are protecting some inward softness that just wants to be handled (or hugged) with love.

Forgiveness is the Kindness that repairs our broken hearts.

Forgiveness in Action

Like most practices related to personal development, the idea of something is typically easier than the execution of it. To "separate the person from the behavior" sounds simple, but it is incredibly difficult because our woundedness, anger, resentment, and personal feelings are deeply attached to the experience.

If we could approach life with all the tools and wisdom offered by gurus and guides, we'd all be living in individual and communal harmony. The objective strategies and sayings are all available to us. Life, however, tends to be quite personal. Which is why we can fully *comprehend* something and still be quite bad at *living it*.

The practice of forgiveness is a bedrock for Kindness in our most personal relationships, including the one with ourselves. Resentment, bitterness, jealousy, or any of the numerous emotional ailments that forgiveness can help cure are like the fly you spot on the movie screen—once you see it, it's hard to take your attention away from it. Though the movie continues on in the background, we can't tear our eyes (or our hearts) away. And, of course, our attention amplifies the bad as effectively as it does the good. When we grow angry, it colors all we do toward a person. How am I supposed to be Kind to someone who I believe to be wholly untrustworthy, callous, or ignorant?

With most of these competencies, it is worthwhile to start with the person or people closest to you and ripple out from there. In this case, that first person is yourself.

1. FORGIVING MYSELF:

Brené Brown believes that our self-talk should be as positive and powerful as the words we share with our closest friends. She frames it like this: "Talk to yourself as you would someone you love."[1]

So much of the negative messaging that circulates in our brain is recycled garbage. It is external nonsense that makes its sinister way into our internal beliefs. But because a lot of it is generated from the outside, it helps sometimes to undo it from the outside, too.

Write down a list of two or three damaging things that you say to yourself often. Take a breath. Now share this list with two or three close friends or family and explain that you need their help—that you are working on forgiving yourself and need some backup from people who might be able to see you from a more flattering angle than you sometimes see yourself. If they are willing, request that they share how they see you differently from these messages you have been saying so often internally.

Then, after gathering a few responses, sincerely ask yourself if you trust these people you asked. Try accepting, just for a day, that their perspective could be just as true (if not truer) than your own.

2. FORGIVING THOSE WHO HAVE HURT ME:

Think about someone in your life toward who you are holding anger or resentment. If possible, think about what primary action this person took to cause this damaged relationship in your life.

In your mind's eye, separate this person from their behavior. Carefully visualize the *action* that caused you pain as its own entity. Then, distance the deed-doer from their deed. Now, let's make it less abstract. I want you to think about what potential "lagging skills" and "unsolved problems" this person has in their life (see pages 45–46). What skills might they have been missing that would have caused them to behave in this way? What problems were they navigating that might have caused them to act like this?

Try making a voice note to yourself where you make up a new story to the best of your ability. Tell the most compelling story you can imagine as to why this person would ever behave the way they did. Maybe you actually know some of the details, or perhaps they are all total fiction. Either way, sell yourself.

What if, just for today, that person was totally deserving of your love? What if the story you told yourself about this person was so heartbreakingly real and hard that you couldn't help but want to give this person your Kindness?

Disclaimer: This exercise will be harder to do for some behaviors than others. There are some traumas or abuses that need professional help to process and unpack. In those cases, this exercise should not be your first step on your road to healing.

3. FORGIVING THOSE DAILY IRRITATIONS:

While we all have some deep wounds in need of healing, most of our opportunities for forgiving live in little daily moments of frustration. The slow driver when you're in a hurry. The shouting baby when you happen to have a migraine. The person texting and not paying attention when it's their turn in the long line you've been hungrily waiting in.

David Foster Wallace's poignant commencement speech in 2005 sets the stage for this conversation well. In the address titled "This Is Water," he says:

> "The point is that petty, frustrating crap like this is exactly where the work of choosing is gonna come in. Because the traffic jams and crowded aisles and long checkout lines give me time to think, and if I don't make a conscious decision about how to think and what to pay attention to, I'm gonna be pissed and miserable every time I have to shop. Because my natural default setting is the certainty that situations like this are really all about me. About MY hungriness and MY fatigue and MY desire to just get home, and it's going to seem for all the world like everybody else is just in my way."

If we don't pay attention to *how we think* in these day-to-day situations, our life can easily be quietly ruled by what he would call "petty frustrations."[2] When we make ourselves the center of all these situations, our capacity for Kindness is diminished. When we choose to focus exclusively on our personal anger or irritation, we become a prisoner to our own perspective.

Forgiveness is freedom because it offers fresh insights into familiar patterns. What if we always gave ourselves permission to at least try on a more generous lens?

Brené Brown shares that, in all her research, the people who are hardest on others are often hardest on themselves. She challenges herself (and her readers) to spend time to truly consider the world through this humbling point of view: *everyone, at all times, is doing their very best.*

Spend the entire day today trying to consider everything and everyone through this perspective. Offer each person you cross paths with the internal generosity of "they are doing the best they can." Catch yourself in the act of any moments of judgment or doubt and make the deliberate choice to forgive and forgo those passive, daily, petty frustrations.

THE KIND OF KINDNESS THE WORLD NEEDS . . .

is one with forgiveness at its foundation. If we are unable to free ourselves from our own self-recriminations and resentments, we will never be able to give with the generosity we are capable of. The writer and activist Adolfo Pérez Esquivel puts it plainly when he says, "We cannot sow seeds with clenched fists."

Resentment is a painful preventer of progress when it comes to our personal generosity and the fullness of our love. If we are to sow seeds of Kindness, we must open our hands and our hearts to the possibility that every person's story is forgivable—including our own.

4

[INSECURITY]

*T*he insecurities we have about ourselves are barriers to our connection with others. Rejection, failure, embarrassment, and shame are not physical monsters under our bed, but they are monsters nonetheless. They are scary in their remarkable ability to prevent us from living life fully in love with ourselves or others. They stand in the way of making bold and caring choices. They suffocate self-compassion and, in turn, reduce our personal capacity to give.

A monster like shame whispers, "You aren't smart enough to make a difference," and stops your helpful brain before it has a chance to start. Failure can prevent you from reaching out to someone if it can make you think you won't do well or won't know what to say. Embarrassment might keep you from standing up for someone when it shouts, "What are people going to think?" or "They are going to laugh at you next!"

Courage, it is important to remember, is not the absence of these monsters. It is not fearlessness. Rather, it is the decision to confront the things that scare us the most. Courage is the choice to turn on the light so we can more accurately acknowledge and consider the monsters that are naturally scarier in the dark. Unacknowledged fear is the scariest sort because it makes decisions in the background that profoundly affect the foreground. We've all missed out on opportunities for love because we were afraid.

Deep Kindness requires courage. It requires you to reflect on the things that terrify you so you can make decisions from a place of consciousness instead of cortisol. Courage doesn't destroy fear; it simply gives us the freedom to choose a life less encumbered by doubt and worry. Courage helps untangle and more thoughtfully observe our insecurities. The exercise of courage starts with awareness and works its slow way toward autonomy.

Insecurities Are the Fears We Believe In

I've spent most of my life scared. Not necessarily a heart-pumping kind of fear, but the slow-building, life-corroding rust that builds up over time and weakens the likelihood of you realizing your dreams.

We think of fear often as an active thing—something that triggers us into fight or flight when we *feel* terror, horror, or repulsion. We think of fear as something we run from; ironically, it is something we often run toward.

There is a comfort in fear that we rarely acknowledge. If I come to believe that I am not capable of doing something or living a certain way, then there is self-satisfaction in living out my self-imposed limitation. If I doubt myself capable of action and then *don't act*, I just proved myself right.

And we all like to be right. Especially to ourselves.

We are not conscious of most of these internal conversations. Our brains like to make a lot of subtle computations in the background without bothering us in the foreground. In any given circumstance, our minds are measuring (usually without our explicit permission) the level of risk involved or our personal ability to overcome the odds. We can't help but think about how we might be perceived, how other people's opinions might shape the outcome, the likelihood of our failure, and on and on.

Most fear isn't active. It's passive programming that dictates our everyday choices by telling us what's possible, prudent, or positively idiotic. It's a small but persistent voice that speaks in absolutes like "never" or "always" or "good" or "bad."

"I could never do that."

"I always screw stuff like this up."

"They are good at this and I am bad at it."

Fear is the ultimate salesperson and a chronic liar.

That's how I've started thinking about insecurities in my life: lies we come to believe as truth. Insecurities are the fears that have sold us. They are the make-believe monsters that we've convinced ourselves are real.

Most of the things we are afraid of are simply lies that we've been told (or told ourselves) so often that we've started to believe that they are true. Think about all the inputs you receive on any given day. *Forbes* concluded that the average person is exposed to five thousand ads in twenty-four hours.[1] In 2011, *Fast Company* found Americans took in five times as much information every day as they did in 1986.[2] There are over 21,274 television stations in the world producing eighty-five thousand hours of original programming every day. YouTube gets six thousand hours of video added every hour. My phone just told me my average screen time this week went *down* from last week to a mere five hours, sixteen minutes a day.

Some valid questions: Is this information serving my best interests? Does it benefit my internal dialogue or the picture I hold of myself? Is all this information even true?

When we are bombarded by so much data, it becomes quite difficult to know which morsels we are digesting and which we aren't. We can't *decide* fast enough what is worthwhile or honest, so we end up taking in a lot of trash alongside some treasures. Our brains aren't inherently equipped to sort information on such a large scale. All this information coming in isn't measured objectively as true or false. It isn't stored based on its merit or accuracy. It is evaluated and kept, most often, by the strength of our *feelings* around it.

When something hurts us deeply, our brain doesn't respond, "Yeah, but that's categorically untrue."

It usually asks, "What if that *is* true?"

Maddeningly, most of these measurements are happening outside of the conscious mind. Over time, we start to adjust our life to these subjective data points and begin to believe things in our brains that affect our way of being. Think about all the lies you've been told since you were a kid. Broad-sweeping cultural programming tells us all kinds of things that we didn't necessarily sign up for—we have to achieve, get good grades, and get accepted into a good school. We have to have a good, well-paying job and drive a certain kind of car. Real men do this and real women do that; boys like blue and girls like pink. These messages, and millions of others like them, are embedded in that constant inbound data, and we can only filter so much of it.

While our cultural programming happens *near* us, our most personal programming happens *to* us. The kindergarten bully who told you that you were stupid and small. The fourth-grade girl who broke your fragile heart when she stopped paying attention to you. The father figure who was supposed to be your rock but was instead your hell. The teacher who told you to stop making art because you weren't any good.

When we are told directly or indirectly that we are supposed to be a certain way or we should never be another way, our brain unintentionally listens. It gathers all that information and builds a self-preservational operating system around it. Then, without our fully conscious permission, we begin to *live* based on these *lies*. Our Kindness toward ourselves and others is shaped by these insecurities in both large and small ways.

When rejection, failure, embarrassment, or shame start playing a role in our decisions, Kindness gets harder. Incompetence isn't the only barrier; just because we know *how* to do a thing does not guarantee that we aren't *afraid* to do that thing. That is why just cultivating competencies is not enough for a Kind life; we must also cultivate courage.

My parents showed me *The Lord of the Rings* far too early in my life. The horribly tragic and saggy-skinned Sméagol character scarred me at the ripe age of six. I would picture him lingering in the dark corners of my room or at the bottom of a staircase when the lights had just been turned off downstairs. To this day, when I flick that final light switch off, I sprint up the stairs.

I know I'm not the only stair-runner out there. We all know the feeling of fear creeping up our neck that causes us to run from unseen monsters.

Those moments of active fear cause most of us to run from things like spiders or a Sméagol. It is the quieter fear—the more passive, subtle, pervasive fear—that causes us to run from things like Deep Kindness. Or perhaps even walk slowly by Kindness as three thousand people did in the airport with Helga.

When we are scared of something, we will avoid it. We will run up the stairs and away from courage. Only a thoughtful acknowledgment of these fears can begin to free us up for more meaningful and consistent Deep Kindness.

This whole section on the insecurities born of fears is designed to remind us that Kindness can be scarier than it sounds. It creates a compelling case for the courage we must cultivate to overcome the monsters of our mind.

So let's start with one of our favorite fear monsters: rejection.

Chapter 13

REJECTION—NOT-SO-FREE HUGS

*I*f you've ever been on the internet, you've probably seen a video of someone giving out "Free Hugs." Most of the clips feature heartwarming scenes of smiling faces embracing in various locales. The final cuts rarely show you all the moments that people denied the squeeze. They almost always give you the highlight reel of happiness—the distilled joy of strangers connecting.

I've offered Free Hugs in a few locations: at a mall, on downtown streets, in Central Park, at Pike Place Market, at the homecoming game for my alma mater. Let me tell you: it is primarily an exercise in rejection.

Most people have a parentally nurtured and healthy aversion to strangers. These scare tactics usually involve candy and kidnapping. When it comes to Free Hugs, it's not just the fear of strangers that keeps people away; most people are in their own world with their own friends and, if they aren't immediately taken with this out-of-place embrace, then the vast majority of them will walk on by.

If people walk by when a smiling stranger is offering a hug, just imagine how easily people walk by a suffering stranger like Helga offering heartbreak.

The repeat rejection of Free Hugs can very quickly cause you to throw in the towel. Our brains are wired to protect us from pain, and each time someone waves you off or pretends like you don't exist, the most natural reaction in your head is, "Wait, why am I doing this?"

• • •

Whether you've held a Free Hugs sign or not, we've all had these small moments of rejection or refusal in the face of our own offers of personal generosity. Perhaps you invited someone to an event you thought they'd love, and they didn't even respond. Maybe you offered a compliment or a gift, and it got laughed at or dismissed. Have you tried to talk to someone who seemed lonely and they stonewalled or totally ignored you? Perhaps you've offered a sandwich to someone who appeared to be in need, and they demanded money instead?

It doesn't take many of these moments to make you cynical or sour toward the idea of helping someone. Each rejected moment of Kindness chips away at your resilience to repeat the act. There are few things more heartbreaking than wanting to do something *good* and getting something that *feels bad* in return. It's the contrast that hurts: you are trying to be Kind, and instead you get kicked in the gut.

Of course, you don't need to simply be rejected in a moment of Kindness for rejection to still *affect* your Kindness. Fear cross-trains all the time. The rejection from the school play or soccer team will impact your fear of rejection elsewhere. The primitive part of the brain that considers these moments of pain isn't detail-oriented. It paints fear with a broad-stroked brush. You don't have time to think through all the details, so your brain just generously reminds you of *all* the times you've faced anything like rejection as soon as you are about to do anything that might have the same result.

Thanks, Brain. Your discernment leaves something to be desired.

I was speaking many years ago at an alternative high school in Washington State. The small crew of kids who go there are there for reasons that span a hard-to-hear spectrum. They come from broken homes and broken systems. Some are readjusting fresh out of juvenile detention and some just can't stand to be in a traditional classroom. Some are gang members; some have been ganged up on.

These tend to be my favorite audiences to work with. The prominence of suffering in their life almost always brings empathy closer to the surface. They know, better than most, how to help someone who is hurting, because they are experts on the subject of pain. Few things can replace lived experience.

I spoke for an hour about Kindness and the barriers we face with it. I talked about our personal capacity for change and the power we wield each day to influence the world. I left time for questions at the end because, with a group like this, there is always a really healthy and curious skepticism. Some of them feel like their world hasn't been Kind, so why should they?

Near the front, there was a kid with a metal necklace, black cargo pants, and his hat in his lap. His hair still had imprints from his cap; I could tell he would rather have kept his head covered, but the school had its rules. He raised his hand and, with full sincerity, asked, "What if people don't want my Kindness?"

I could tell this was a question rooted in hard experience. This kid had faced a lot of rejection in his life, even in his honest attempts to help.

We dug in for a while, back and forth. I prompted him to share some examples and he spoke of people cynical of his sincerity. He talked about moments when people downright denied his offers to step in or step up. I asked him why they might doubt his motives and he shared that he had a reputation for hurting people in the past. I responded by asking him if anyone had ever tried to offer him Kindness, and he said, "Yes, the same people that took it away." I asked him who he trusted in his life and he said, "No one."

It was an upsetting reminder that, for many people, Kindness can actually be a precursor to pain. Most, if not all, of us have had people in our lives who were Kind, but then one day did something that was anything but. There are people around us every day who are desperate for Kindness but too terrified to receive it.

This kid had seen others' selflessness turn into selfishness, yet he still had something to give. I could tell he was close to the end of his hope. He was on the precipice of a life committed to cynicism because the world had provided him with no evidence that anything else was worthwhile or trustworthy.

Eventually, we arrived here: "Perhaps it's not that people don't *want* Kindness—we all do. Perhaps they just don't always trust the source it's coming from."

The nature of trust is the reason something like Free Hugs is riskier than the videos make them seem. The people walking by aren't dismissing Kindness so much as they aren't *trusting* it. If the passerby's personal traumas involve any sort of heartbreaking or trust-breaking, consciously or subconsciously, they will avoid that hug at all costs.

Sometimes risking connection is to risk reliving hurt.

To be conscious of this emotional balancing act allows us to offer Kindness more carefully and take rejection less personally. Being rejected when you offer Kindness isn't usually an external commentary on you. It's the recipient's internal reaction to their natural and nurtured fears of abandonment, abuse, and those people in their life who had given them Kindness, only to take it away.

The student came to the conclusion himself: "So maybe it has less to do with how good I am at Kindness, and more to do with me working to be trustworthy again in people's minds?"

He was exactly right. We can't receive something we don't trust.

To build the trust required for someone to receive Deep Kindness, we must understand the building blocks of trust. People need three primary things: empathy, authenticity, and consistency. Do they believe that you understand them (empathy)? Do they believe that your effort is genuine and rooted in honest intention (authenticity)? Do they believe that your action today is in alignment with other parts of your life? In alignment with what you will do tomorrow and the day after that (consistency)?

Your actions must be free from external expectation and feel authentic in your desire for the highest good—not your ego or what you may get in return. In some situations, you must prove to me that you mean it by showing up again and again. "Am I a one-off event for you or do you care enough to return? Will you be Kind to me on my bad days alongside the good? Am I the recipient of your pity or am I worthy of your ongoing efforts?" Consistency is crucial for trusting connection because time is priceless. Deep Kindness is an exercise in attention allocation.

The majority of people who move us deeply only have the ability to impact vulnerable parts of our heart because they've earned the necessary trust to operate such high-level controls. You wouldn't trust a new employee to manage the most sensitive data, would you? Sometimes we forget that giving and receiving Kindness is, for many, an intimate and personal experience. In order to truly deliver Deep Kindness in a way that sticks with people, you must ask meaningful questions and exercise the skill of listening in a way that makes them feel heard. "Do you know me well enough to be Kind to me?" is a question that *I*, the doubtful or cynical recipient, might ask.

Listen well. Be humble and self-aware of your intentions so your actions are rooted in integrity. Show up, and then show up again. And then show up when they least expect you to. These are the ingredients of trust.

Take, for example, the grade-school "Kindness classic" of sitting next to the kid who sits alone at lunch. In attempting to sit with this person, we are (1) making an arbitrary assumption that this person *wants* our help, (2) implying that *we* are the ones whose company they desire, and (3) asking for the receiver to be in close proximity with someone without any level of pre-built or earned trust.

Don't get me wrong, there are examples of this sort of cafeteria compassion going well. We should definitely check on people who truly look like they are having a tough time or seem disconnected from their community. However, to leap into the lunch seat next to a stranger and assume that your mere presence is going to change things is at its best arrogant. At its worst, it reinforces why this kid wanted to sit alone in the first place. Can you imagine going through a hard time, having a kid you've never met drop in next to you with a big smile and lots of questions—and then never sitting with you again? It would do nothing but confirm that people don't *actually* care. It would feel like their attention was just an assignment or a "random act," but not anything authentic.

It's an opportunity for Deep Kindness that often gets replaced by Confetti Kindness, and the results can be damaging.

The person who goes to sit next to the lonely kid thinks they are doing a good thing. And, for most, they *are* well-intentioned. However, after the initial ecstatic greeting, the conversation can get terribly awkward because there is no history before this moment. It's a one-way, forced connection without two-way permission. Meanwhile, your friends are at a table nearby and they are laughing and having a ton of fun. To make it worse, the kid you've sat with starts to ignore you. To reject you. *You!* The one who just came to keep him company.

That is when we can get a little indignant. In the hurt of our rejection, we claim the moral high ground.

I sat next to you and you didn't want to talk to me?

I offered you a sandwich and you wanted money instead?

I tried to give you hot chocolate and you said you were lactose intolerant?

I am doing a *good* thing. How dare you reject *my* act of Kindness!

There is an unintentional arrogance that can arise when we believe we are doing something good. We naturally believe that the way we give Kindness is the way everyone will want to receive it. That the time when it is most convenient for us to share it should be the precise moment when others are ready to receive it. We can hold an unconscious expectation that everyone should be grateful for what we give because it has a personal cost to us.

When the expectation for what you get in return for Kindness becomes personal, you're in for a lot of disappointment. Conditional Kindness—the kind that demands gratitude or acceptance—almost always serves you more than the person on the far side of your ego. This is what can happen when we reduce an act requiring Deep Kindness to the convenience of confetti.

THE KIND OF KINDNESS THE WORLD NEEDS . . .

is one that is free from the expectations of what you get in return, rejection or otherwise. It is the kind that can outsmart our own brain and declare that Deep Kindness is worthwhile, even though it might result in pain. It's the kind that can distinguish between our personal hurt and our prevailing passion.

The kind of Kindness the world needs acknowledges that rarely is Deep Kindness received without some level of trust. Even the action of giving Free Hugs can cost the recipients *comfort* in order to receive them.

We must work to become more trustworthy so that our Kindness can be received (without the expectation that it should be).

Rejection Reflections

The incompetence section has practical exercises to help build up muscle groups that aid in the actions of Kindness. While incompetence can be overcome with rehearsal and repetition, insecurity is best navigated first through reflection. These reflections are designed to help you overcome various insecurities in an effort to gain enough courage to achieve Deep Kindness.

Here are some prompts to use to journal, ponder, or converse with friends to help us overcome the lies that get in the way of love:

- What moment of rejection stands out most in your life? How do you think it's affected your Kindness?

- Do you accept Kindness from others well? Why or why not?

- With which groups or people do you think you are perceived as most trustworthy? With which do you think you are perceived as least trustworthy?

- When do you expect things in return for your Kindness? When has your Kindness been truly free from expectation?

- What rejection are you willing to face today to be Kind?

Chapter 14

FAILURE—ELEVATORS, VULTURES, AND THE TERROR OF NOT DOING IT RIGHT

"It is a risk to love.
What if it doesn't work out?
Ah, but what if it does."
—Peter McWilliams

The fear of failure is an internal cost/benefit analysis between the price of caring and the potential helpfulness to the human on the other side of our choices. What if I invest time or energy into this person and they dismiss me? What if it doesn't make any difference? What if I don't know what to say?

What if I give all of myself and nothing happens?

Ah, but what if something does?

You probably do not need any more lectures on failure. It's a hot topic in cultural conversations today; we all know that the most successful people built their fortune or fame on a bedrock of "I blew it"s. We know Michael Jordan had to miss a lot of shots in order to make the ones we remember. We know that garage-built companies like Apple were laughed at before they were lauded. We have all heard, in just about every podcast or book on *winning*, that you gotta first *lose, lose, lose.*

Overnight successes happen over the course of ten years. The world's finest athletes train during hours when the rest of us sleep. Hard Work + Opportunity = Luck. You know the drill.

Dr. Angela Duckworth, who wrote the book *Grit*, shifted many paradigms with her analytical discovery that our traditional metrics of success—GPA, IQ, SAT—were actually less important than the less commonly discussed quality of resilience.[1] She discovered that those who were most successful had a common denominator: they were willing to fail. They stumbled forward through the wreckage even when things felt most wrecked. While others floundered in their failure, they forged ahead and, eventually, flourished. Success is almost always less about navigating arrival and more about navigating adversity.

Similarly, success in Kindness is dependent on our willingness to face failure. There is no guarantee that an act of Kindness is going to work or help someone in the way we might hope. More important, if we fear failure in other parts of our life, it's likely we will avoid the adversity that is sometimes required to engage with others in those messy moments of Deep Kindness. What if I don't know what to say or do? What if I say the wrong thing? What if I plan this event and no one shows up? What if I put in all this work and don't get the results I believe in? If we aren't willing to risk these things going wrong, they'll never have the chance to go right.

This fear of failing in Kindness is either dismissable or deeply personal. Let's say that my fear of failure drives me away from helping a stranger. My brain can self-justify this failure because the results (or lack thereof) are too abstract to even understand. I can walk by Helga in the airport and, without knowing her name or story, I can minimize the stakes. The less responsibility I feel toward a person or idea, the more I can dismiss failure as inconsequential.

"I'm sure she's fine."

"I bet someone else is coming to help."

Our disconnectedness from the narratives or needs of most people makes it easier to ignore acts of Kindness directed toward the strangers that surround us. If I don't see why failing this stranger matters, then my helpfulness is like a tent in the wind: without stakes, it's easy to blow by most opportunities for generosity. If there is even a sliver of hope that "someone else" will help, my brain can rest easy that this person isn't my burden to carry.

In psychology, this concept is called "diffusion of responsibility." It's a lot like farting in an elevator: the more people available to blame, the less likely you'll be held accountable. So, let it rip.

In Kindness, failure is more often about inaction than action.

Diffusion of responsibility is one of the core justifications for the Bystander Effect—the more people present in a situation with a person in distress, the less likely people are to help the distressed person. In the 1960s,

Bibb Latane and John Darley studied these concepts in depth through a variety of experiments. Here is the most straightforward data to interpret: In 1969, they found that 70 percent of people would help a woman in distress when they were the only witness. When other people were added to the equation, only 40 percent offered help.[2]

When someone else could potentially help, we have less accountability to do it ourselves. Elevator farts.

It is the observation of failure that is so contagious. When other people around us fail to react, we take this as a sign that a response isn't needed or isn't appropriate. Researchers have found that people are less likely to intervene if the situation is ambiguous. If they don't really know *how* to help, *who* to help, or *why* they should help then, well, they probably have better things to do. No one likes to take a test they didn't prepare for.

Most of the time, the unknowns involved in these situations feel so distant or abstract that they are easy to dismiss in order to get back to being busy and living our own life. Sometimes, though, these failures can come back to haunt us.

You may already know the story of Kevin Carter. He was a photographer during apartheid in South Africa, and he'd seen enough heartbreak to overwhelm even the most hardened souls. In 1993, he flew to Sudan to capture images of the famine happening at the time. After a long day, he headed into the bush and stumbled upon an emaciated toddler who had curled up and collapsed on her way to a feeding center. Just as he was about to take the picture, a massive vulture landed nearby. Carter had been told not to touch the people because of rampant disease, so, instead of helping, he waited twenty minutes, hoping the bird would leave. It stayed.[3]

At that moment, he captured a Pulitzer Prize–winning photo.

He eventually scared the bird away but remained distant from the child. The image was a foundational case study in the debate over when and where photographers should intervene. In July of 1994, Carter took his own life. The note he left behind wrote, "I am haunted by the vivid memories of killings and corpses and anger and pain."

It's impossible to know if Kevin Carter killed himself because he couldn't shake his anger, sadness, or guilt. Perhaps it was some combination of all three.

What we can reflect on is our own relationship with his story. Carter's narrative calls to mind a challenging prompt: When was the last time my failure to be Kind was personal?

For me, it looks a lot like a voice message.

I was at Leadership Camp deep in the woods with no cell service. It's a real gift to have that many people disconnected for a week, but as it turns out, it wasn't a great week for me to disconnect.

While away at camp, one of my best friends lost his mom to ovarian cancer. His name is Lucas. His mom's name was Cindy.

One of the first messages he sent was to me. It was a voice memo that had the tone of someone who had exhausted himself crying. Like the world had punched him in the throat.

"Hey, man, just wanted to let you know we lost Mom last night."

As a staff member at camp, we get very minimal nighttime internet access. Most things don't come through, but this note did. I didn't get it until near midnight and, expecting one of Lucas's usual silly, sardonic notes, I didn't brace myself for pain.

The voice memo played and my breath caught. I put my hand to my mouth and left the room. Under a crisp night sky riddled with stars, my heart broke for my best friend.

For *four months*, I didn't pick up the phone to call him.

Perhaps it's because my job involves speaking thoughtful words that I feel a greater pressure to say the perfect thing in moments of consequence. I'm worried that I won't say the right words or be able to help and, as a best friend, it feels like that's supposed to be my job more than others who exist on the periphery. Acquaintances can more acceptably send their "my condolences" and say "I'm sorry for your loss," but my call had to be so much more.

I was so scared of failing my best friend in his moment of greatest hurt that I failed to act at all.

Voltaire said that perfect is the enemy of good.[4] In this case, my desire to "help perfectly" was the enemy of any action entirely. The more time that passed, the more I felt stupid for not helping. I had first failed at saying something comforting or Kind and then I began to worry I would fail at explaining my absence in a way that would justify it.

I allowed myself the self-serving excuses of "I'm busy" or "He's busy." I texted back and forth and tried to set up a call but didn't follow through. I'd even deluded myself into the narrative that "he'll reach out when he needs to."

In December, over one hundred days after the initial voice message, I went to see Lucas perform at a comedy show. The jokes about his mom's passing were, for him, so evidently heartbreaking and heart-healing. We drove back together and I steered the conversation toward trivial things so I could avoid the tragic. We arrived at my house and got out to hug. The air was heavy with the unspoken mess that I desperately wanted to untangle. It was like pulling out a treasured necklace that had sat in the drawer for too long that's now riddled with knots and you have no idea where to start the unraveling. Lucas took a step back and held me in a quiet gaze of patient love. I knew that *he knew* I wanted to say something and he patiently waited for me to sort out my sadness.

Stepping through my fear and shame, I stumbled through it. "I'm sorry," I said. "I apologize for not showing up for you as your best friend. I know that's my role and I know that I was supposed to call and I was supposed to be there and I haven't been. At all. Like, worse than at all because I haven't even acknowledged how I haven't shown up. I've felt like such an idiot. The truth is I've been feeling incompetent and insecure and I've avoided the whole thing. Repeatedly. I'm sorry, Lucas. I love you and I am so dang sad about your mom."

I'm crying. His face, lit by the moon, was gentle and Kind. He put his hand on my shoulder and smiled through his own tears. "Houston, what you did hurt. I gotta tell you, it was hard that you didn't call. That you weren't at the funeral." He took a breath, resolved and compassionate, and went on, "But listen, I understand. I forgive you, buddy, and I love you."

That was it. My fear was suddenly transformed into admiration in the clear generosity of his forgiveness. Thank you, Lucas. You make me better.

I can't stand feeling helpless. I'm not sure anyone really loves the feeling, but I associate many of my most painful memories with that distinct and dastardly emotion. To watch people I love (and myself) suffer and not feel capable of doing anything to help seems like the ultimate failure. And sometimes the risk of feeling helpless will prevent me from being helpful at all.

I don't know if your failures (or your fear of what it means to fail) look like mine. I do know that, for most of us, failure in all its forms rarely *feels* good. Unfortunately, to care about a stranger or a best friend almost always carries with it some level of potential failure: that you won't have the "right" words to say; that you'll save someone from starvation but not malaria; or that you couldn't possibly be the best person for the job when there are other, more capable people around who won't screw it up.

So, in quiet moments or in loud rooms, we walk by opportunities for Kindness. We walk by Helga at the airport. We avoid the call. We don't step in, step up, or send the message we've been meaning to send.

Pick up the phone. The fear of failure is the false story that people expect your goodness to be flawless. But as it turned out, Lucas just wanted my presence—not my perfection.

THE KIND OF KINDNESS THE WORLD NEEDS . . .

is the one that willingly accepts helplessness. It's the kind that acknowledges that no effort toward compassion will ever be perfect. The imperfect action of Kindness is almost always better than the failure to act at all. The world needs people who are willing to fail—not just in their business plans or in their athletic pursuits, but in their efforts to serve. To give. To love.

Failure Reflections

Here are some prompts to use to journal, ponder, or converse with friends about that may help you navigate the fear of failure and how it holds you back from being Kind:

- When was the last time you failed someone close to you in Kindness? What can Kindness look like with them today?

- How has the Bystander Effect affected you personally?

- How are helplessness and failure connected in your life?

- How might you redefine success for yourself in such a way that you'd be willing to face failure for it?

- When was the last time you succeeded for yourself? When was the last time you failed yourself? What does Kindness toward those moments look like today?

- Who has failed you? What can Kindness look like toward them now?

- What act of compassion is so meaningful to you that you're willing to fail for it?

Chapter 15

EMBARRASSMENT—
TO DANCE WHEN EVERYONE IS WATCHING

I've always wanted people to like me. Perhaps most of us feel this way, but I'm not sure we are all affected by this need to the same degree. The depth of this desire has a strong correlation to how often or how painfully you've been mocked or dismissed along the way.

At my fifth birthday party, a neighbor kid came over uninvited and pushed me down from behind and split my top lip open over the concrete. It was the first time I felt humiliated, and it happened to be on a day that was supposed to celebrate me. The embarrassment of bleeding all around your cake table can't be understated. At age five, you can't understand why someone would want to hurt you. It's impossible to wrap your head around the fact that this action had nothing to do with *me* and everything to do with something *he* was navigating in his own life.

The kid was ironically the child of two neighborly Buddhists who believed in nonviolence. Apples sometimes do fall far from the tree. This one felt like he wasn't even in the same orchard.

In first grade, I was standing with my back against a giant tractor tire on the playground. A group of kids, most of them older and bigger, made up a game where they would throw wood chips at me and assign different point values to different parts of my body. I imagine you can gather what numbers went where. Needless to say, it wasn't my favorite game. I transferred to a new school to get away from the embarrassment.

In the fourth grade, I tested into a class of fourth, fifth, and sixth graders in a new elementary school. It was a three-year program that put me in the "honors" student track. I remember students non-affectionately calling us the "Nerd Herd." My near hour-long bus rides were rather miserable.

I've always felt a bit different from the world. My fads and phases haven't always lined up with culture's timing. I have a deep desire to stand out that comes, ironically, from a deeper desire to be accepted because, at so many junctures along the way, I haven't been. My efforts to be seen and known have created natural targets on my back. After all, the animal that roams from the herd is the first to die.

If we agree with Helga's assessment that "Kindness isn't normal," it's a humbling reminder that the action of Kindness is then, by default, *different*. Weird. Unusual. And any time we step outside the circle that our world has decided is "normal," we risk being laughed at or humiliated by those inside the circle.

Kindness, then, almost always risks embarrassment. To stand up for someone that a group has deemed "other" naturally associates you with the "other." To offer help to someone that everyone has passed by opens you up to passive resentment—an unconscious judgment shaped by people who don't want to admit they weren't willing to make the Kind choice first. The majority of people *want* to help, but resent the minority who *actually do*.

And Deep Kindness, unfortunately, is an action of the few. We will always judge most harshly the things that we aren't ready to do ourselves.

Early in my speaking career, I was at a high school near my hometown. After the assembly was over, it was time for lunch. There were seven hundred people in this big, round cafeteria and the kids were shuffling to their seats. It was a Spirit Day and I found my way to a table that looked like they had extra pizza on hand.

The kids at the table willingly shared a slice and one of them, a bit mature for his age, asked, "What happens when you get old and your stuff is no longer relevant?"

Super good question. I remember not having a good answer.

A few minutes into lunch, as people got settled, the student leaders started playing music over the cafeteria speaker system. First track: Michael Jackson's "Beat It."

Many students are adept at ignoring most things in school. This was no different; lunch went on as usual. Except for one student, a ninth-grade boy on the far side of the cafeteria, who stood up determinedly from his chair and started to dance.

His move was rather unforgettable. I wish I could show you in person, but if you can, picture someone getting up and down out of a chair with their hands straight by their sides. Like a skinny string bean of a kid doing half squats in a straitjacket.

There he was, bobbing up and down, and I watched as heads started to turn. It was the delayed reaction of a school that was used to being in their own lunch table world. One by one, people started to take notice of this bouncing young boy. One by one, kids started to point. And talk among themselves. And *laugh*.

I could tell they were mocking the kid, but the kid just kept on dancing.

I was cringing as I watched this unfold. My empathy was firing on all cylinders, feeling for this poor dude who must have felt humiliated.

Nearby, the student body president, a girl named Christina, hopped out of her chair. It wasn't showy; she just made her deliberate way to the far side of the room, reached out and offered her hands (he accepted, awkwardly), and began dancing with him.

Not her own moves, mind you. She joined in the sitting-string-bean situation right with him.

It felt like an eternity watching the two of them bopping up and down while the rest of the room laughed. I remember thinking to myself, "I would *never* do that."

It was an odd internal declaration because I love to dance. When I was five years old, my dad pulled me aside at a YMCA dance where I wasn't dancing and shared with me a life lesson that would shape many of my formative years.

"Houston, girls love a guy who can dance."

I've spent the last twenty-five years trying to figure out if that was true.

I really love to dance and I remember stumbling over my own internal dialogue as I watched these two kids.

"I would never do that." I was confused at my own assessment: "Why not? Why *wouldn't* I do something that I *love* to do?"

Of course, my empathetic concern for these kids had nothing to do with their dancing. My resistance to what I was watching also had nothing to do with my personal willingness to boogie. What I was honestly horrified by was the idea that I might do something I love, while seven hundred people *laughed at me* in return.

Tiny moments of embarrassment add up along the way to shape that kind of fear. If you put music on in front of any group of little kids, they will all dance. But at some point along the way, most of us get told that our movements aren't right or our rhythm is all off. We learn that other people's approval is paramount to our fitting in and, one by one, kids start to stop their dancing. One by one, we start to sit down—not because we stopped loving to dance, but because we became increasingly aware that someone was watching. Judging. Laughing.

I've realized how often in life I stay seated when I'd rather dance. In fact, most people in the world will live their whole lives in their seats (and do not even realize they're doing it). Why? Well, it's certainly safer there. It's easier to be the one laughing at the person dancing than it is to be the person dancing. So, we shrink our uniqueness into conformity. We acquiesce and adapt. We play it safe and small and we tap our toes to the beat in place of a dance we gave up a long time ago.

I'm not sure when it happened for me. At what point along the way did my fear of being embarrassed *become bigger* than my love of dancing? When was the moment that I gave up what I cared about in the face of what I was scared of?

And the more challenging question: Where else in my life is that true?

Where else in my life is my fear of being laughed at larger than my willingness to love? Where else is what I'm afraid of *bigger than* what I believe in? Where else in my life do I say I want to dance, but instead I stay seated?

How many times has my fear been bigger than my Kindness?

Here were these two kids dancing. Seven hundred people laughing at them. And they just wouldn't stop.

Two nearby girls hopped up and crossed the length of the room. The duet seamlessly became a quartet.

Another three. Another four.

When the group hit about twelve, they moved from the outskirts to the inskirts. They formed a circle in the center of the room, and they kept dancing.

I watched as the table closest to them confronted the weirdness unfolding in front of them. At first, they wanted to play it cool. You could see the whole table recoil in defense and look at each other like, "This is dumb."

But proximity is powerful, and a few more students had joined the group in the center.

You could see the decision-making spelled out on their faces: What happens if I join this thing now? Will it keep growing and become cool or will I be laughed at like the rest of them?

We tend to only acknowledge the early adopters of something when it all works out. But for every victorious product, there are hundreds of failed ones that had plenty of full-fledged fans.

The table looked at each other and, in silence, questioned: "If I do it, will you do it?"

They literally counted down and, all at once, their table of eight joined in. There is power in numbers—tackling embarrassment together makes for a lighter burden than dealing with embarrassment alone.

It didn't take long for other tables to see where this thing was inevitably going. The tide had turned. The majority had become the minority faster than they could come up with any resistance. And all of a sudden, seven hundred people were dancing in that cafeteria around this scraggly-haired, squiggly-dancing kid.

Not just students. The teachers were bouncing. The lunch servers were boogying. The principal was on a nearby table, breakin' it down.

The boy in the center had a funny look on his face, a mix between joy and horror. I think he was happy to be dancing, but a little terrified that it had taken off quite so quickly. What a gift, I thought, to operate in a way that is different from so many. Maybe it was his neural networking—a brain that didn't process, like the rest of us, the social programming that might otherwise tell him that his dancing might be perceived as weird or ripe for humiliation. His was a brain that offered him a freedom that so many of us seek: to not consider (in the same way) the flimsy opinions of others when it comes to doing things that we love.

Or perhaps it was simply courage: the choice to rise above embarrassment in favor of the things we care most about. To make your passion, belief, love, or Kindness *bigger than* your fear is the action of the brave.

Courage is not fearlessness. It is the decision to dance when it is scariest.

I'd be remiss if I didn't mention the girl. The first one to hop in next to the odd man out. The first person who was willing to step up against embarrassment, knowing full well she'd be exposed to some secondhand suffering. To dance alongside this kid, not knowing if anyone else might dance with them. To absorb even a few stares or laughs so that he didn't take all the damage.

In Latin, the word "compassion" means "to suffer with." To walk into the fire with someone, knowing that it's going to burn.

To dance when everyone *is* watching.

THE KIND OF KINDNESS THE WORLD NEEDS . . .

must be decidedly bigger than embarrassment. It takes a stand, knowing with absolute certainty it's more convenient to sit. It's the kind that is willingly different when it's easier to be normal. It accepts the humble position of the minority when it would be far easier to cozy up to the majority. It steps up beside others who are suffering, knowing that the burden of judgment is best carried with company.

It's the kind of Kindness that operates from caution-to-the-wind confidence, believing that if I dance long enough, perhaps I can convince the whole world to dance with me.

After all, the animal that wanders from the herd may be the only one to discover that the grass is greener where no one else is trampling it.

Embarrassment Reflections

Here are some prompts to use to journal, ponder, or converse with friends about in order to help us overcome embarrassment's grip on our goodness:

- When is the first time you remember being embarrassed or humiliated? How has that shaped your actions throughout life?

- Where in your life is your fear bigger than what you care about?

- What action can you take to overcome this fear?

- What has caused you to "stop dancing" along the way? What would get you dancing again?

- When have you willingly signed up to be in the minority? Why?

Chapter 16

SHAME—THE SCARCITY OF "ENOUGH"

> *"Shame is the most powerful, master emotion.*
> *It's the fear that we're not good enough."*
> —Brené Brown

I wish I could pinpoint the moment when I started feeling less than *enough* in my life. For some of us, I imagine it's crystal clear—a moment of trauma or pain so specific and incisive that it cuts right to the epicenter. I'm inclined to think that all of us are predisposed to soft spots of sensitivity. Just as we were born with soft spots on our heads, we have them on our hearts. And some of us have the unlucky misfortune of finding people in our lives who take advantage of those most tender fears. Some of us, all in one devastating moment, can suddenly come to believe that we aren't worthy of love.

For many of us, we are just quietly programmed by culture to believe that we simply aren't *enough*. We need better grades; we need to be about three inches taller. Your chest isn't burly enough and your stomach isn't flat enough. Your job doesn't make enough money, your house isn't fancy enough, and your photos don't get enough likes. You're not smart enough, beautiful enough, fast enough, or successful enough.

You get the point. You know the point. *Enoughness* is in rare supply. Culture simply doesn't benefit from people feeling abundant, so it tells us a different story. And who are we to argue with culture? How can the story we want to tell ourselves possibly compete with the story being crafted by the best and brightest, the companies that profit off our doubt, and the overwhelming majority?

What happens when we don't feel like we are *enough*? What happens when we believe that we are unworthy of love, attention, or kindness? The tragic by-product is that we give up on the possibility of connection, joy, and change.

"Shame corrodes the very part of us that believes we are capable of change," Brené Brown writes in *I Thought It Was Just Me*.

Shame is perhaps our deepest source of hopelessness. It is our darkest voice, whispering all the things you don't want to believe are true, but . . . what if they are? It speaks in hypotheticals that sound like absolutes.

Shame is external commentary turned internal criticism. It is a lie that once upon a time came from the outside and, now that we've repeated it for so long, we only hear in our own voice. This subtle shift from "You" to "I" is among the most damaging transitions we could experience.

"You'll never be as good as them" becomes "I'll never be good."

"You're useless. You're a burden" becomes "I deserve to be alone."

"You need to do better. You're a disappointment" becomes "I'm not enough."

You become the star witness, the prosecution, and the executioner. After all, there is no one who knows you better than yourself. There is no better testimony than a confession.

And so you indict yourself to what could be, without careful consideration or intervention, a life sentence. The perpetual punishment of *being* someone who lives their life believing they are less than. A life without the courage to dance. A life of diminished love.

When you live from this place—when your actions are driven by shame and scarcity instead of hope and abundance—you consistently prevent yourself from finding opportunities for connection, authenticity, Kindness, and joy. Hopelessness is effort's greatest enemy, and effort is a critical ingredient in any act of Kindness.

Living from a place of shame drives one of two primary ways of avoiding intimacy—retreat or relentlessness. Some run away from responsibility, while others bury themselves in it. We've all tried on both options and we probably fit more snugly into one more than the other. Some find themselves running away or shutting down when they feel most helpless or incapable. If you ignore a limb long enough—if you sit on your leg for enough time—it'll start to go numb.

Many of us run toward a never-ending to-do list that keeps us busy long enough to arrive at exhaustion. And in exhaustion, in that sweet state of spent-ness, we have no more energy to hurt. The numbness of inaction is different than the numbness created by overexertion, but they both have the same outcome: we get to *get out of* feeling.

Of course, numbness is nondiscriminatory. It doesn't distinguish between happiness and hate. It doesn't know the difference between pain and purpose. It's just a circuit breaker that turns off the Christmas tree alongside the toaster that's on fire.

When I was navigating my divorce, I dug into a lot of personal development work to try to figure out what the heck was wrong with me. How was it possible that someone who talked about love for his career could be quite so inept at it in his life?

There is something acutely shameful about speaking something like it's truth and living it as a lie. There is something deeply painful about promising something to others that you can't give yourself.

One of the articles I read in the *New Yorker* during this desperate period of self-reflection was about the Four Burners Theory.[1] The framework is rather simple: your life is represented by a stove with four burners. Each burner is symbolic of one major piece of your life.

- The first burner is your family.
- The second burner is your friends.
- The third burner is your health.
- The fourth burner is your work.

Let's say that, like time or effort in our life, this stove has a limited amount of gas. The implication then is this: in order to be traditionally successful in work, you have to turn off one of the other burners. In order to be "really successful," you have to cut off the gas from two.

This concept offered me a simple framework for self-reflection. I felt traditionally successful in work and it was obviously at the expense of, in some ways, my marriage. Let's call that the family burner. As a result of my busy schedule and the crises I was facing in my romantic relationship, I'd spent a few years without much time for my friends. I would get the texts and invites asking to hang out and I'd almost always respond with "on a plane" or "not tonight." Over time, after hearing "No" often enough, my friends just stopped reaching out. There goes the friend burner.

My diet consisted of airport lunches and hotel dinners. My exercise was walking back and forth between the bleachers at the school I was speaking at, before sleeping on my subsequent plane ride. I was exhausted and stressed and overwhelmed. There goes the health burner.

Was the success I'd found at work worth the burners I'd turned off? With all the gas burning on work, one might think I was doing it because it made me happy. Unfortunately, that's not how shame works.

Shame will burn all your gas on gourmet dinners for one hundred guests and still leave you wondering why you hadn't prepared dessert. Shame will drain you of your resources and convince you that you could have done more. Shame is the low-quality fuel that'll slow cook your soul before it ever warms the soup.

When your productivity is rooted in shame, it keeps you persistently *doing* without the reward of ever feeling *done*. Busy kept me numb to navigating all the most complicated emotions in my life. And in the shame spiral that kept me working toward a success I'd never really feel, I found myself disconnected from all the things that gave my life true meaning: connection, intimacy, depth, and Kindness.

Deep Kindness thrives on time and attention and effort. It requires gas. And I'd all but shut it off in every aspect of my life except for my work.

My work had become the vehicle for shame. It was the most acceptable avenue for me to play out my "never enough" narrative, because the harder I worked, the more people applauded. From all external vantage points, I was making a difference and finding success. This surface-level success played well for my audience, but it was ravaging my heart. Perceived success makes the shameful person comfortable in their numbing because their performance is evidently working. It's only when we finally step offstage that we realize how exhausted we are from playing a part we didn't intend to audition for.

Of course, we all have seasons in our life where we will be busier in one burner than another. But if we don't have the tools to diagnose where and why our time is going the places it is, we can easily end up spending our most important currencies—our attention and effort—in places dictated by our *shame* instead of by our *self*. Once I had the tools to self-reflect on my unbalanced burners, I was able to start the long process of reprioritizing my world. It took me three years to move from one hundred and twenty nights on the road to seventy. It's not as simple as turning the stove on or off, but the disciplined reorienting of my schedule has been worth the work. I've been able to dance more, cook more, and RSVP with an enthusiastic "Yes!" to the surprise of many friends.

THE KIND OF KINDNESS THE WORLD NEEDS . . .

is one that leans into the fullness of all feelings—even those that most terrify us. It's the kind that gives from a place of abundance and enoughness. A Kindness that isn't deadened by the numbness of self-avoidance, but vibrant with the wholeness that comes from self-acceptance. A kind that is alive with the intensity, clarity, and bounty of attention that only comes from a full and loving balancing of *self* so you can properly allocate your burners to others. Deep Kindness operates from the wholehearted perspective that there's not *enough* time for everything, but you are *enough* in everything you do.

Shame Reflections

It's reflection time. Here are a few prompts to use to journal, ponder, or converse with friends. These are designed to allow us to thoughtfully confront shame and its efforts to corrode connection and Kindness:

- What part of you feels incapable of change? In what way does it reduce your capacity for Kindness toward yourself or others?

- What is something you intentionally numb and how does the numbing of the negative reduce any areas of positive?

- What burners have you turned off in your life? How has it affected your Kindness?

- Has there been anything you've read so far in this book that has made you feel less than *enough*? Is there any other way to frame the story you're telling yourself?

- Where do you feel abundance in your life and where do you feel scarcity? Reflect on each of these ideas and their relationship to Kindness.

• • •

Fear is scary to fully feel. Healing is not something we arrive at overnight, but something we chip away at like layers of paint on a graffitied wall. Full healing is dependent on full feeling, and that process of chipping away can take months and years. The depth of our courage will be directly related to how truthfully we acknowledge and confront the monsters that affect us daily—in the dark and in the light. You don't defeat demons by ignoring them—you have to wrestle them and accept that you may have to fight the battle more than once. The more challenging fight may even be to forgive and befriend them.

This whole process takes energy and time, which can be terribly inconvenient. In fact, most of the efforts and exercises required for Deep Kindness are an inconvenience for our otherwise already busy lives. Is it worth our precious time? Will we settle for complacency or will we embrace an inconvenient pursuit?

5

[INCONVENIENCE]

I had just finished an assembly at a high school in Texas when a senior boy walked up to me. He was wearing a school jersey that his family had obviously bought one size up. There was a backpack on his back and another bag slung over his shoulder that carried his gear. He was evidently off to practice soon and carrying the weight of all this baggage with a clumsy grace born through repetition. His long hair flowed about as well as his words. "After listening to you today, I realized I'm a really nice person."

I laughed. Sometimes it's tough to know when high school kids are giving you a hard time. It seemed as if maybe this was one of those situations where his friends had dared him to give me some false praise and see how I'd react. Or maybe he was going to explain to me that what I was doing didn't make a difference and people were just going to be whatever they were and why was I even bothering wandering around the country's schools?

It wouldn't have been the first time that some disheartened kid had tried to get my attention by attempting to dishearten me, too.

I responded with, "That's great! I'm glad you feel nice, because that was sort of the point of today," and turned to engage with the other kids waiting in line.

He held out an arm that felt a little shaky with determination, like maybe he was making himself more vulnerable than he realized with this conversation. He stopped me before I could shift my attention and said, "No, you don't understand. I realized over this last hour that I'm nice, but I'm not very Kind."

"What do you mean?"

I'm a word guy. Color me intrigued.

"Houston, everyone thinks they are nice, but that's because nice is easy. It's reactive. You know what I mean?"

I nodded my head in encouragement. This kid had been rolling this over in his brain the whole last hour. The tumbler in his mind was sloughing off the hard edges and the grime. There was something precious here, he knew.

I did, too.

"It's like, people will help others here at school when it's convenient for them. When it's easy. It's just a reaction, you know? If someone is nice to you, you'll probably be nice back. If you agree with someone, you'll probably be nice to them. If you see someone drop their stuff and you're gonna get something in return like bonus points or their number, you'll probably go and help them."

I laughed to myself. A handful of memories flashed through my brain of all the moments when I was extra Kind because I thought maybe a cute girl was looking. Maybe those moments were actually more nice than they were Kind.

He continued, getting more and more animated. "But, Houston, as soon as it's not convenient, comfortable, or you're not getting something out of it, that's when the whole system breaks down at our school. No one wants to do anything that doesn't help them, too. We have to assign community service here. Everything is about a stupid popularity contest, and if it doesn't get your attention, it's not worth doing. When you talked about Kindness today, I bet half this room dismissed you right away, thinking to themselves, 'I'm already a good person, why do I need to listen to this random guy?'"

Ego triggered. Always a healthy reminder as a speaker that just because you're talking to a quiet room, it doesn't guarantee anyone's listening.

"It makes me so angry! People will just ignore this stuff and then complain about why school is such a mean place. Everyone here would say they are nice, but then proceed to keep up the same stupid stuff that makes our school hard to show up to in the first place."

He makes a good point. I've always been more effective at complaining than habit changing. Most of us have fallen into that ego trap before. We'll say we like to take the high road, but then we'll grumble about the construction. We will look down on the low-roaders and loudly boast about the superior view.

"Houston, man, I think nice is easy because of how reactive it is. Kindness—I don't know, the way you talked about it today made so much sense—it is way harder. Kindness is proactive."

"That's brilliant," I said. This kid was on a roll, and I wanted to know more.

He blushed a bit—a funny sight for an otherwise confident kid who was about three inches taller than me—but forged ahead.

"Kindness doesn't have the strings attached. It doesn't wait for something to happen; it makes things happen. It goes out of its way to look for people who need help, and then figures out the best way to help them. You shouldn't have to have someone be nice to you first before you are Kind to them. You shouldn't even have to agree with someone to show them they are worthy of your Kindness."

I want to take this kid on the road with me.

"Houston, why do we always wait for people to drop things before we make them feel helped? Why do we always have to wait for bad stuff to happen before we finally figure out why it's important to make people feel good?"

He was getting teary-eyed at this point. You could tell something in his heart was never going to be the same. For whatever reason, some story or idea I'd shared that day helped unlock something he had been thinking and wrestling with for a long time. When storytelling works, it helps polish diamonds that were already there. When an outer story intersects with an inner one, new connections form between old pieces of a puzzle we weren't sure we had all the parts for. These moments of unearthed wisdom are the most privileged and meaningful moments I get to witness in my work. They are the Big Events. These exchanges are precious, and I've learned not to take them for granted.

"You said today that Kindness isn't normal in the world. Well, I don't think it's normal for me either. And I really want it to be. I want it to be the default way I interact with the world, and I realized today that Kindness actually requires a lot of work . . . and I think I have a lot of work to do."

"Yeah, man, me too." I nodded my head. "I've got a lot of work to do, too. I think we all do."

I hugged him. I gave him my gratitude. I told him thank you for seeing something so brutally in plain sight and yet so far from our shared practice. I urged him that his revelation was a gemstone worth sharing and one not to be kept in some fragile shadowbox tucked away in the garage.

We all know Kindness is important, but not everyone wants to do the work. Everyone thinks they are nice. And I think that's dangerous.

Why? Because niceness can be the demeanor of the dismissive. Nice people can have the attitude of people who've already arrived: "I'm a nice person" leaves little room for growth. The nice person need not improve because they believe they're already there.

The nice person isn't always self-reflective. They often assume they're helping others, when they are mostly helping themselves. Have you ever seen someone get defensive when someone doesn't accept their niceness? "How dare they! I'm doing something nice for them!" is the reaction of pride, not generosity.

The nice person has a countenance based on convenience. They will act one way around you and potentially a very different way around someone else. They'll say, "What a nice dress!" with a plastered-on smile, and then make fun of you behind your back. They'll help pick up trash after a long night—but only if someone is watching so they can get the credit.

It is a dangerous thing to believe we are doing good for the world when we are primarily doing good for ourselves.

It is easy to confuse nice and Kind. We sometimes use them interchangeably, but understanding the difference between the two is crucial for a better world. Confetti Kindness can sometimes be niceness masquerading as something meaningful.

Nice is unproductive. It doesn't move the needle forward. It doesn't shift the status quo.

Why? Nice is easy—it is reactive at its best and self-serving at its worst.

Nice is easy because it is "I"-oriented. Do *I* have time? Do *I* like you? Do *I* feel like it? Do *I* have anything to lose?

Kindness is different—Kindness is proactive.

Someone doesn't have to drop something in order for us to lift them up or encourage them. Something bad shouldn't have to happen in order for us to practice making people feel good!

Where nice is "I"-oriented, Kindness is heart-oriented. It says, "We all need attention and appreciation. We are all deserving of generosity and hope." It moves beyond feelings and conveniences. It is a deliberate choice to bring encouragement, support, or appreciation to yourself or others.

When we align ourselves with the deep purpose of Kindness, it motivates action even when we don't "feel like it." Growth, improvement, and expansion are expensive—and the biggest costs are convenience and comfort.

Nice steps back, while Kindness steps up. Nice happens when there is time; Kindness happens because we *make time*. Nice expects something in return, while Kindness is free from expectation.

To put it simply: nice people don't change the world, but Kind people can. Nice is pleasant, but doesn't usually require much pain. It is non-sacrificial and, as such, rarely makes a lasting difference. It can scratch an itch, but it won't resolve the rash.

The reality is that most actions in Kindness are wildly inconvenient. It almost always costs us something—time, effort, comfort, pride, ego—and very rarely do we actually *feel* inclined toward those losses. And *feelings* play a rather large role in our *actions*.

That's what this whole section is about. It suggests that most of the feelings that we feel on any given day (and there are lots!) don't lend themselves to acts of Kindness. If I don't *feel* like doing something, there has to be a pretty compelling case to get me to do it.

How can we possibly have a Kind world when, most of the time, it's just not all that convenient to create one? How can we create a Kinder world when, most of the time, we simply don't feel like we *have* the time to make a difference?

Chapter 17

BUSY—MAKING TIME FOR LUNCH NOTES

Have you ever gotten news so bad that your body stops working right?

I was standing in the kitchen having just finished a bowl of Life cereal and getting ready to walk out the door to speak at a school when the phone rang. It was still early in the morning—before seven a.m.—and it was my aunt's number coming through. I felt a spike of anxiety because this was an unusual combination.

"Houston, honey, your mom just finished up her colonoscopy—"

I didn't even know she was going in for one.

"—and they found what the doctor believes is cancer."

My back was suddenly against the sink cupboards. My legs had given out, and I was shaking like the garbage disposal had been turned on.

"I'm so sorry, Houey. We will figure this out."

She put my mom on the line. I don't think I've ever thanked my aunt for being the courageous and Kind messenger that day. I know all about tough phone calls and I'm grateful she didn't hesitate.

I know you don't know my mom, but you should. She's one of a very small group of people in my life that I genuinely believe everyone in the world should meet.

I'm an only child and a total mama's boy. She's always been a role model and hero to me—the epitome of the kind of Kindness I'm talking about here. Maybe I should have titled this book *Be Like My Mom: The Story of an Only Child Who Turned Out Okay*.

My mom packed my brown paper bag lunch until the last day of my senior year. Some might find that silly, but acts of service are my love language because it provides the irreplaceable gift of time. High school was overflowingly busy for me, and her daily lunch packing gave me space and time to accomplish all the things coming at me at once. I was able to invest fully in my education because she prioritized the pastrami so I didn't have to.

You could almost always count on a sandwich on a hoagie roll protected by tinfoil. A small pack of chips. Some veggies or some raisins. One of those Talking Rain sparkly waters from Costco.

And a Post-it Note.

Every day, she would write something. A word of the week. Or a quote. Or just a little reminder that I was loved.

Honestly, when I first dreamed of writing a book, I thought it would be called *Lunch Notes from My Mom*. I know I mentioned earlier that Post-it Notes are, in some ways, the kind of Confetti Kindness I'm fighting against. But let me be clear: these notes weren't generic pleasantries passed out at random. My mom wrote something specific and thoughtful, and she never missed a day.

There is something understatedly beautiful about small consistencies—about the tiny things that are done so relentlessly over time that, when added up, they actually equal the biggest demonstrations of love. Pastrami and Post-it Notes. That's the stuff that matters most to me when I look back.

I cried a lot after getting off the phone that morning. Unsure of what else to do, I got in my car and drove to the school I was supposed to speak at that day and delivered my message the best I knew how. I let the school know at the end what was going on. They agreed to be on video yelling, collectively, "Choose love and kick cancer's butt!" I'd record that same message fifty more times over the next three months at every school or event I worked at.

It turns out the doctor was right—my mom did indeed have cancer. Not only in her colon, but in her liver as well. It had metastasized, which meant it was Stage IV. I couldn't not google it. And I couldn't not cry.

Sometimes simple black-and-white information tells you a story you're not ready to hear.

What I didn't know was that my mom had been putting off her routine colonoscopy for over a year because she *didn't have time*.

> If you are putting something like this off for any reason, please, on behalf of my mom and on behalf of the people that care about you and on behalf of yourself, get your butt checked. Make the call today. In fact, if you need to, put this book down right now and do it.
> I promise I'll wait.

There was this profound and irritatingly incisive article a few years ago in the *Wall Street Journal* called "Are You As Busy As You Think?" It begged us to consider the way that we speak to ourselves about time.[1]

What if we were never again allowed to say, "I don't have time"? What if we had to say, "This is not my priority," instead?

"I don't have time to go to the doctor" becomes "My health is not my priority."

"I don't have time for this conversation right now" becomes "Our relationship is not my priority."

The things we give our time to are the things that we value. Our most finite and important resource is time, so where we put it is indicative of what we care about.

Unfortunately, we are addicted to a certain way of using our time. By choice and by circumstance, we are obsessed with being *busy*.

We don't need to belabor the point long made throughout this book that, for many of us, our worthiness is wrapped up in our busy-ness. Productivity is a primary pathway to a sense of purpose and lovability. Our culture tells us that success is a metric most commonly measured by profit, ROI, and getting stuff done. As a result, our to-do lists loom large and drive the economy (and our lives) rather exhaustingly forward.

Capitalism is a cultural freight train and we usually realize at some point along the way that we ain't the conductor. In fact, most of us are tied down to the tracks with some cartoonish bandit character looming above us, laughing in the back of our mind that we're doing this whole thing wrong but we can't quite figure our way out of the ropes.

This whole driving economical and societal force of "busy" is actually one of the most common disconnectors of Kindness. In fact, one of the most frustrating studies on the subject happened in the 1970s at Princeton Theological Seminary School.[2]

They took a small group of students into Building A and explained to half of them that they were going to be preparing and delivering, in just a short period of time, a speech on job opportunities in the seminary field just across the way in Building B.

They told the other half of the students in Building A that they would be giving a practice sermon on the parable of the Good Samaritan. It'd be delivered shortly on the other side of the quad in Building B. The story of the Good Samaritan is, at its core, a story of stopping to help strangers in need. Perhaps you see where this is going.

Two very different kinds of talks: one of them a presentation on career paths, the other an impassioned sermon on helping people.

In between Building A, where they had time to prepare, and Building B, where they were supposed to deliver, the researchers planted a stranger along the route who was obviously in pain and evidently in need. They wanted to know: Would the people actively *thinking about compassion*—those literally about to talk about stopping to help strangers—be more likely to stop and help this one?

The short answer? No.

The longer answer: the biggest determining factor in whether or not people stopped to help—whether en route to deliver the service-oriented sermon or the seminary slide deck—had mostly to do with how *much of a rush they felt like they were in.* How much time they felt like they had to get from Building A to Building B.

Do you ever feel like you're in a rush between Building A and Building B?

It feels like sometimes in between Point A and Point B, we are entirely capable of missing the point.

My mom went through eleven rounds of chemotherapy. She had a colon resection and 70 percent of her liver removed at Mass General Hospital by one of the best surgeons in the world.

After the liver removal, she spent seven days in the hospital. I got to be there for the whole stint, and, along the way, she had a whole squad of people coming in and out of her room assigned to her care. I probably met at least twenty different people throughout the week, and you know what I find interesting? I only remember one of them.

Her name is Wonderful. It's not her given name, but it's the one she gave herself.

I asked her why she went by Wonderful, and she said matter-of-factly, "So many people told me I was wonderful, I just decided to call myself it."

She was immediately my favorite. She would walk in singing and walk out dancing. She had skin the color of a cloudy night and eyes that held you tighter than a hug. One day, Wonderful and my mama were trying to take a few steps down the halls of Mass General. After a big surgery like this, they want you up and moving as quickly as you can muster the strength. All of a sudden, Wonderful starts singing "The Sound of Music." I have no idea how or if she knew that my mom had been the lead in her high school's production, but Wonderful was belting it out with my Maria-Mama and it didn't take me long to realize that Wonderful didn't even really know the words.

It didn't matter. My mom took twice as many steps that afternoon as she had in any other attempt.

My mom, as of this writing, is currently three years cancer-free. In 2018, we traveled to Uganda with students and got to work with schools—a twenty-year Bucket List item she had never made time for. She got to celebrate my thirtieth birthday with me. I just celebrated her sixtieth with her.

I think about her time at Mass General often and have spent a lot of time reflecting on why I remember Wonderful over anyone else. All the nurses were competent and generally caring. They all had a similar set of responsibilities: manage IV lines, administer medication, report to the doctor.

It has since occurred to me that you can do everything you're *responsible for* at work and not be memorable at your job. Doing something well isn't the same as doing it wonderfully. Why? Well, you can accomplish everything on your to-do list without ever really prioritizing the Who You Want To Be List.

Wonderful fulfilled her responsibilities, but you could tell that playfulness, encouragement, and warmth were top priorities. She took these abstractions and made them daily actions. Competence and Kindness are not mutually exclusive and they require an equal attention to detail.

We all want to be Kind. Present. Grateful. Good listeners. Humble. Forgiving. But the laundry, our inbox, and the project proposal on a deadline all feel a little more tangible. More checkoff-able. And if there is one thing we love in our current culture, it is getting things done. Sometimes we will even write down something we've already done, just so we can have the satisfaction of checking it off.

Our To-Be List is a bit more amorphous than our to-do list. It's certainly less traditionally productive. In business, we tend to measure all the things that matter, but there isn't a spreadsheet for selflessness. There's not an effective accounting system for altruism. So, we tend to stay busy with what we know needs to get done and hope we already are or will eventually just *become* the Kind, generous, patient people we have always wanted to be.

Unfortunately, our To-Be List requires just as much practice and work as any other skill or success in our life.

As Will Durant tells us, "We are what we repeatedly do. Excellence, then, is not an act, but a habit."[3]

Ironically, to *be* a thing, we must repeatedly *do* that thing. It becomes a *matter of time*. Will you make time for the practice of gratitude? Will you prioritize singing "The Sound of Music"? Will you design your schedule around service and not just strategy meetings?

My friend Dexter Davis once told me, "We are all human becomings."

In order to *become* the traits we have always wanted to *be*—Kind, or something like it—we have to reprioritize what we *repeatedly do*. We have to acknowledge "busy" as the never-ending excuse that it is—a vague cultural peer pressure that keeps us so buried in bottom lines that it prevents us from being anything but surface-level successful. The metrics of our character aren't as easy to measure, but they still matter very much.

The kind of Kindness the world needs is the kind that is acknowledged as so crucial that we are willing to prioritize our precious time to make the practice of it real. It's the kind that shifts our schedule around to make sure we can sing. It's the kind that acknowledges that the greatest resources we can allocate in our lives are our minutes and our moments, and knows that our most profitable and productive investment will always be in the hearts of others.

Every day we can choose to sacrifice even just a few seconds to the practice of being Kind. Confetti Kindness happens on occasion, while Deep Kindness happens consistently. It maintains a thoughtful awareness of the ongoing time that must be dedicated to *becoming*. Maybe it's in a daily check-in we have with a friend who is struggling. Perhaps it's an extra minute each morning to send a message of gratitude toward three people in your life.

Maybe it's something as simple as a meaningful daily note in someone's lunchbox.

In fact, I think that'd be rather wonderful.

Chapter 18

EXHAUSTION—
OVERCONSUMPTION AND OVERWHELM

I've had the airport sweats more often in my life than I would like. Running from Terminal A to Terminal K is a horrific sort of hustle when your last connecting flight is on the line. There's no substitute speaker option for me if I'm not there, so if you miss a flight to one destination, you sometimes have to hop on a different itinerary and strap in for a long drive.

There has been more than one occasion where I've pulled into the school with thirty minutes of sleep before trying to entertain a few hundred middle schoolers. Sometimes the time change isn't in my favor, my body is under the weather, and I have to speak to not one, but two schools that day. Usually, I'm hopping on another plane to head to another state right as I finish up at the second campus. I know I just got done talking about the risks of being busy, but I also know from very personal experience that we sometimes just want some third party to acknowledge that our schedule (no matter how self-imposed) seems totally nuts.

There are so many people in this world whose lives, by necessity, are insanely busy. People whose very survival (or the survival of their family) is dependent on a frustratingly endless sprint. Systemic poverty and oppression set people up for the single-parent, three-job storylines that will inspire you while they break your heart. And these sorts of unreasonable calendars are not just reserved for adults. You can walk into high schools today at their seven thirty a.m. start time and you see a scene out of *The Walking Dead*— the average teenage schedule is packed more tightly than most CEOs'.

People of all ages are exhausted. This results in two primary consequences: (1) you are so sleepy that you become snappy or downright mean, or (2) you don't have the energy to give to anything because you're in survival mode. Deep Kindness costs something, and if you don't have money in your emotional bank account, you typically go into penny-pinching conservation instead of philanthropic generosity.

Over 40 percent of Americans don't get enough sleep. The average time of sleep per night has decreased an hour over the past sixty years. Studies show that sleep deprivation is correlated with a disconnect in the part of the brain responsible for keeping emotions under control.

"It's almost as though, without sleep, the brain had reverted back to more primitive patterns of activity, in that it was unable to put emotional experiences into context and produce controlled, appropriate responses," says researcher Matthew Walker, director of the University of California Berkeley Sleep and Neuroimaging Laboratory.[1]

Our lack of dream time makes us less than dreamy to be around. Kindness comes less easily to those who don't have the energy to give it. However, our nighttime routines are not solely to blame for this exhaustion. Our busy way of life provides a certain soul-grinding, sleep-depriving byproduct. The diversity of experiences we encounter every day is another attribute to blame for making us feel so run-down—the sheer amount of data our brains have to process sets the stage for feeling overwhelmed. The barrage of information we receive daily leads to an exhaustive experience in emotion.

The diversity of content we consume is wildly different than what we had access to a hundred years ago. As a result, in a single minute online we might see images of our ex, videos of puppies playing, and headlines about some international tragedy. All in a span of a few seconds of screen time, we can feel jealousy, joy, and devastation.

Sometimes we aren't even aware that we've felt all those things. The rate at which we can consume content today doesn't always match the rate at which our brain can understand how that content affects us. So we either end up feeling passively exhausted because our bodies can't keep up with our brains, or we numb ourselves unconsciously to combat an indigestible diversity of drama.

In either case, Kindness gets harder. In fact, most of the feelings that we feel on any given day don't lend themselves to the practice of Kindness.

Take a look at the short list of feeling words in the *How are you feeling?* chart on page 132. It is organized roughly by the intensity or depth of the emotions inside of a few feeling categories. The expansion of our emotional vocabulary is an intentional practice and can help us better understand what we are actually experiencing instead of defaulting to more basic, umbrella words like "mad," "sad," "glad," or "afrad" (*afraid*, but the rhyme helps me remember).

These distinctions are important! The categorical imperative to "eat your veggies" is quite different from the nuance of knowing which veggies to eat, how to prepare them, and how they impact your body. Our emotional menu and our ability to navigate it is similar; the specificity with which we are able to identify our feelings gives us greater control over how those feelings shape our actions and deepens the understanding of what we are experiencing moment to moment. "Knowing yourself," Aristotle says, "is the beginning of all wisdom." With vegetables and Aristotle in mind, use the chart to ask yourself some reflective questions:

- What feelings have you felt today, consciously?

- What feelings do you think you've felt, consciously or unconsciously, because of content you've consumed?

- What percentage of this whole list of words are feelings that make Kindness "more likely"? Which of these feelings make Kindness more challenging?

- Which of these feelings do you think are most pervasive in our world today? Why?

How are you feeling?

MAD	SAD	AFRAID	GLAD
IRRITATED	DOWN	STARTLED	RELAXED
ANNOYED	DISCOURAGED	WORRIED	CONTENT
TENSE	DISHEARTENED	INSECURE	SECURE
JEALOUS	APATHETIC	STRESSED	HAPPY
FRUSTRATED	SULLEN	ANXIOUS	HOPEFUL
DISAPPOINTED	MOROSE	FRIGHTENED	PROUD
RESENTFUL	LONELY	REJECTED	PLAYFUL
HATEFUL	ASHAMED	EMBARRASSED	CONFIDENT
LIVID	DESPONDENT	ALIENATED	OPTIMISTIC
INFURIATED	DEPRESSED	INFERIOR	ENTHUSIASTIC
ENRAGED	HOPELESS	INADEQUATE	INSPIRED
	DESPAIRING	OVERWHELMED	ECSTATIC
		TERRIFIED	JOYFUL
			LOVING

INTENSITY

If you aren't paying attention, you can easily find yourself stuck in the land of Mad, Sad, and Afrad. The emotional selection here is not typically where you want to live, but culture seems to put you there with frequency. Culture wants you busy all the time, and your unconscious obedience leaves you exhausted. Capitalism wants you feeling like you are not enough because scarcity is a selling point. Without the proper defenses, you'll find yourself irritated, overwhelmed, insecure, or altogether numb. If this becomes your modus operandi, then most of life becomes about self-preservation. At scale, this leaves us trapped within a broken system with Kindness on the sacrificial altar. The exhaustion of our survival mentality makes selflessness a luxury.

THE KIND OF KINDNESS THE WORLD NEEDS . . .

is one dedicated to its practice regardless of what we're feeling. It's the kind that has decided that the action of Kindness is less dependent on our emotional state and more dependent on a deeply contemplated understanding of need. If we can still show up and be productive at work, at school, or in the world even when we are run-down, overworked, or exhausted, can we find a clarity of purpose that might allow us to show up for Kindness, too? Can we have our own personal revolution where purpose overthrows productivity in the competition for the energetic investment of our lives?

Chapter 19

FIGHT VERSUS FEELINGS— PURPOSE FUELS PERSISTENCE

Kaedan showed up to the front door of his school an hour before the first bell and held the door open for students as they walked in. Over the course of his last two years of school, he never missed a day.

Sometimes it was quite cold. Sometimes Kaedan had been up late the night before, studying after a long afternoon of practice. Sometimes students would laugh at him or totally ignore him. But, determined to exercise Kindness through just this small act of service, Kaedan kept showing up.

I had the chance to work with Kaedan at Leadership Camp for a few years after he graduated high school. I asked him if showing up at the door every day felt hard. He laughed and just said, "It mainly felt early."

There were many days, he said, where he really didn't feel like showing up. I prompted him to tell me what propelled him into action even when the emotions weren't aligned. He responded, "I never wanted anyone to feel lonely like I did."

Dr. Angela Duckworth, in her research on grit, discovered that the most common denominator of the most resilient individuals was that they had a deep, clear purpose.[1] They knew the exact motivation behind what they were doing, and that clarity of cause was the primary fuel in their tank to do their thing even when it was challenging, uncomfortable, or inconvenient.

I never wanted anyone to feel lonely like I did.

Kaedan's statement is rooted in empathy and is definitively more profound than just setting a goal to "be Kinder" or even "to stand at the door every day." If we don't know the *why* of a thing, the *what* or the *how* quickly gets flimsy. The willpower to practice something like Kindness doesn't come from a natural wellspring of altruism, but rather a clear mission that must be cultivated. Discipline is often just as much a function of purpose as it is effort.

Most of our daily feelings don't actually lend themselves to something like Kindness because so many of them focus on productivity, survival, and self-consciousness. How is it, then, that we can escape this selfish storyline and contribute in meaningful ways to the world? How do we make time for something like Kindness or generosity when, a lot of the time, consciously or unconsciously, we don't really *feel like it*?

The question then becomes: Is what we're *fighting* for in this world bigger than our personal *feelings*? Most people make decisions based on what they feel at any given moment. Our emotions drive most everything. Our sadness. Our happiness. Our anger. Our jealousy. And, if most of our actions are driven purely based on how we feel, then our lives are roughly the size of ourselves. We are living for nothing larger than our own emotional whims.

But, if we can manage to carve out some time—to sit down and really consider our purpose for being here—there is magic in it. When we get really clear on what we are fighting for, and we decide that our fight is bigger than our feelings, we can more frequently align our actions to our altruistic aspirations instead of our ephemeral emotions.

To adapt a quote from G. K. Chesterton, "How much bigger your life gets when you make yourself smaller in it."

THE KIND OF KINDNESS THE WORLD NEEDS . . .

is the kind worth fighting for. It's the sort of Kindness that disregards comfort in favor of the common good. It's the kind that transcends momentary trials in favor of long-term love. The kind of Kindness we need today acknowledges that the compassionate world is not a passive by-product of hope, but an active, daily, resilient battle that is hard-won. It flows, in the most difficult moments, from a self-dug well of clear purpose. Deep Kindness declares its fight much larger than its feelings and then aligns its actions each day to make for a winning round. It shows up at the door each day because it holds out hope that perhaps someone will feel a little less lonely because of it.

6

[CONSISTENCY]

*T*here are plenty of Kindness calendars, diaries, and workbooks that have some great ideas on ways to practice Kindness in everyday life.

Most of them don't confront the hard reality that, even with a year's worth of individual ideas, we don't seem to be getting the collective traction we need to make a true, systemic difference. Why? Well, if we don't acknowledge the mess, we will find our upper half clean while our feet are stuck in the mud. It's a good headshot, but we aren't making much progress.

The tools of self-reflection (or collective lack thereof) when it comes to Kindness are a missing ingredient in a complicated recipe. There are things that we don't know we are unaware of—competencies that, if we've never been explicitly taught, we end up just "taking what we get." And it's not like we, in our adult lives, are actively looking for classes on emotional regulation or forgiveness. Therapy might help us unpack some of our insecurities, but it's not often that we look at fear through the lens of love; we don't always question insecurity's relationship with our capacity for Kindness.

And, if you are busy, you are certainly not paying attention to all the feelings you don't have time to feel and how they may or may not be disrupting your do-gooding. You don't have time for those kinds of emotional diagnostics. If you are doing anything related to uncovering or clarifying your "purpose," it's almost always career or self-help related.

The work of acknowledging "what gets in the way of Kindness" is sometimes the most challenging, messy, and self-confrontational piece of the emotional maturity puzzle. If we don't know what skills to build, what questions to ask, or what internal clarity is needed to exercise Kindness with full-ness and with persistence, then we might end up stuck practicing Confetti Kindness in perpetuity.

It does feel like a massive undertaking to create a Kinder world. It feels nearly impossible to make something normal in the world that is presently so frustratingly uncommon. How do we make it so that more people stop to help Helga?

Desmond Tutu said that "there is only one way to eat an elephant: a bite at a time."

What does one bite at a time look like with Kindness?

Did you know that 45 percent of our day is built on routine?[1] That means 45 percent of our week is habit-based. Which means 45 percent of our month is habitual. Which means almost half of our lives are spent on autopilot.

People who are most effective at changing their lives, schools, or communities focus daily on small moments instead of the large-scale events. They realize that habits shape everything we do. If 45 percent of your day is habitual, that means that even a 1 percent difference, over time, is going to have a far greater impact than any one-time action.

Take Kaedan Schmidt, who never missed a day at the door. My mom, who never missed a lunchtime Post-it. What will be the one thing you can do relentlessly to start to build your habit of Kindness—your 1 percent change toward a more compassionate life?

Brené Brown makes the paradigm-shifting observation that, across many of her case studies and interviews, the Kindest people actually have the most (and clearest) boundaries. It feels a little counterintuitive that people who say *no* often would be quantitatively more Kind. But it turns out that saying *no* to a lot of things makes their *yeses* that much more meaningful.

The data is a simple reminder that if we try to do *everything*, we will end up doing *nothing very well*.

As this book comes to its conclusion, my hope is to equip you with one habit of Deep Kindness to integrate into your 45 percent. This bite-size integration into your daily or weekly practices will change not just what you *do*, but who you *are*. Our repeated actions shape a part of our identity, and wouldn't it be cool to have the whole world adopt even one habit of Kindness? Wouldn't it be profound to have the world be 1 percent more Kind?

Charles Duhigg, in his book *The Power of Habit*, shares that most habits are created with the same three ingredients: a cue, a routine, and a reward.[2] When we experience a cue (we get home from school or work, we see the fridge, our alarm goes off at four p.m.), it begins a routine (we sit down on the couch and turn on the TV, we rummage through the leftovers, we put on our workout clothes). The routine is motivated by a reward (we get to turn our brains off, we get a quick sugar spike, we feel accomplished by getting out the door to the gym).

In order to create a thoughtful habit that sticks around, you have to get serious about your own cue, routine, and reward when it comes to Kindness. I challenge you just for the next month to keep this book in a spot you'll see daily. Keep this bad boy out in the open and, each time you look at it (cue), execute on the act of Kindness you are about to commit to (routine). You will be doing good for yourself and the world, and you can make time after each action to reflect on and feel gratitude for your practice (reward).

As we near the end of our time together, I want to give you:

1. A FEW EXAMPLES OF IDEAS THAT LIVE IN PEOPLE'S 1 PERCENT.
2. A WAY TO THINK ABOUT COMING UP WITH NEW KINDNESS IDEAS.
3. A LIST OF THIRTY DAYS OF KINDNESS TO GET YOU STARTED.

Chapter 20

INTERSECTIONAL THINKING—
BREAKING FREE FROM CHIPOTLE CHICKEN PASTA

Kindness is a massive concept. It can be wielded in just about every area or relationship in our lives, so the idea of "practicing Kindness" feels about as large and abstract as "practicing sports." There are so many different choices, I liken it to the menu at the Cheesecake Factory. If you've never been, the menu is pages and pages of delicious-sounding options. When we have too many choices, our brains tend to get overwhelmed and we typically (a) settle on something familiar or (b) avoid the choice altogether.

The first time I ever went to the Cheesecake Factory, I finally decided on ordering the Chipotle Chicken Pasta. It was a long and thought-wearying process. But in the end, it was delicious. So each time I go back to the Cheesecake Factory, what do you think I am most likely to order?

Dang right. The Chipotle Chicken Pasta is my MVP (most valuable pasta) and is, nine out of ten times, what I will order.

We do the same thing in our culture with Kindness. Whether it's in the halls of schools or in Hallmark commercials, we see a handful of "Kindness classics" on repeat and, as a result, it's what we will most commonly "order" if we decide to order anything at all.

"Kindness classics" are the Chipotle Chicken Pastas of Kindness—the things you will go back to again and again because it reduces the overwhelming concept of choice.

Some of the most frequently ordered Kindness menu items are Free Hugs, sitting next to the new kid, Pay-It-Forward coffee lines, and raising lots of money for someone who is sick. There are the old standbys, such as holding the door open, giving socks to people experiencing homelessness, and putting the carts away at the grocery store. These aren't bad orders by any means, they are just so popular that they sometimes prevent us from coming up with anything new (and potentially more meaningful)!

My favorite technique to come up with more unique, specific, and impactful Kindness ideas is called Intersectional Thinking. It's a simple structure that provides the necessary constraints to increase creativity. Step one involves brainstorming categories that narrow your focus, so you aren't trying to come up with just any Kindness idea, but one that relates to something targeted.

For example, the category of *People* helps us think about *who* Kindness can be directed toward. "How do I practice Kindness toward my aunt?" is a more helpful question than "How do I practice Kindness in general?" Constraint actually amplifies creativity.

So, think about an action of Kindness that is meaningful for . . .

- Myself _____
  _____

- My Father _____
  _____

- My Mother _____
  _____

- My Family _____
  _____

- My Brother _____
  _____

- My Sister _____
  _____

- Animals _____

  _____

- My Grandparents _____

  _____

- My Aunts/Uncles _____

  _____

- My Children _____

  _____

- Teachers _____

  _____

- My Coworkers _____

  _____

- My Boss _____

  _____

- My Mail People _____

  _____

- My Dentist/Doctor/Pediatrician _____

  _____

- Firefighters _____

  _____

- Police _____

  _____

- Coffee Baristas _____
  _____

- Waitstaff _____
  _____

The list could go on and on. One category is a great start, but Intersectional Thinking gets even more specific by adding another. Let's say a second category is *Time*.

Think about a practice of Kindness that could happen . . .

- Daily _____
  _____

- Weekly _____
  _____

- Monthly _____
  _____

- Yearly _____
  _____

- Over the Course of a Full Day _____
  _____

- Over the Course of a Half Day _____
  _____

- In Ten Minutes or Less _____
  _____

Now, the magic of the method. Intersect these two categories and see if you can come up with an answer for something *in the overlap*. Combine *people* and *time* for prompts like "How do I practice Kindness with my mom daily?" or "How do I practice Kindness in ten minutes or less with my brother?"

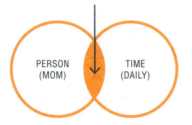

Writing your mom a daily morning text message of encouragement is a different act of Kindness than sending a pizza gift card to your brother, who you know is traveling a bunch this week and won't have time to make dinner. The intention of coming up with these ideas is what helps us move from Confetti Kindness—from the Chipotle Chicken Pastas—into the more targeted and thoughtful realm of Deep Kindness.

You can, of course, add layers to this model. For example, take Gary Chapman's *Five Love Languages*.[1] He says we all give and receive love (or Kindness) in different ways and helps categorize some of these actions into five main practices:

1. **ACTS OF SERVICE**
2. **GIFTS**
3. **PHYSICAL TOUCH**
4. **QUALITY TIME**
5. **WORDS OF AFFIRMATION**

"How do I practice Kindness in ten minutes or less with my brother through Acts of Service?" is different from "How do I practice Kindness in ten minutes or less with my brother through Words of Affirmation?"

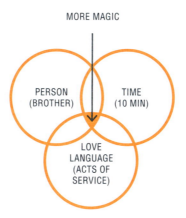

MORE MAGIC

PERSON
(BROTHER)

TIME
(10 MIN)

LOVE
LANGUAGE
(ACTS OF
SERVICE)

The idea to set aside sixty minutes of phone-free Quality Time with your partner after work is a totally separate act of Kindness than adding a new song to a shared playlist with a best friend to give them as a weekly Gift. For some people, the most important thing they can receive each morning before a grueling shift is a thoughtful, intentional hug as they head out the door. It might be the only Physical Touch they receive for hours.

Specificity drives meaning and action.

Think about the difference between receiving a Post-it Note with a generic compliment like "You're amazing!" versus the handmade card that details how you've been influential in someone's life. One might bring a smile, while the other moves you to tears. Why? Because meaningful Kindness is generated from the hard work of meaningful connection.

Don't get me wrong, all Kindness is worthwhile because (as Aesop reminds us) "no act of Kindness is ever wasted." So please don't forgo the coffee Pay-It-Forwards and the happiness of Free Hugs. I repeat: Random acts of Kindness are a beautiful indication of a heart that leans toward love. Random acts of Kindness are the sprinkles that bedazzle the ice cream. But Deep Kindness requires flavor selection, scooping, packing, and (hopefully) a waffle cone. Sprinkles can go on any flavor, but the base is quite a bit more personal.

Why stop at doing good when you are capable of doing great?

Let's make habits of Deep Kindness that are intentional, specific, authentic, and challenging.

Thirty Acts of Kindness

Using Intersectional Thinking as a brainstorming tool, I've created a starter plan for you. Here is a list of Thirty Acts of Kindness that should take ten minutes or less, to help you get out of the Chipotle Chicken Pastas and into a whole new menu. Feel free to customize each recipe to maximize meaning:

- ☐ **MYSELF:** Write down three positive things about yourself on a small piece of paper and put it somewhere only you will see.

- ☐ **MYSELF:** Write down one thing you love about your Past Self, one thing you love about your Present Self, and one thing you love about your Future Self.

- ☐ **MYSELF:** Go for a walk and identify five things you are grateful for that exist within a ten-minute walk of where you live.

- ☐ **FAMILY:** Send a family member a picture of your face smiling and tell them one reason they make you happy.

- ☐ **FAMILY:** Write a short, loving note to two family members and hide them in places that might be hard for them to discover. Text them throughout the day with mysterious hints and see who finds theirs first.

- ☐ **FAMILY:** Make a formal invitation to hang out with a parent or family member. Mark your calendar. Send them a Save the Date and commit to doing something you know they will love.

- ☐ **EXTENDED FAMILY:** Go back through old photos and find a picture of the two of you. Send it to them and tell them why it's a positive memory.

☐ **EXTENDED FAMILY:** Write a post on social media about an extended family member and pretend it is National _____ Day (Uncle, Second Cousin, Great Grandma). Share why you are proud to have this person as a part of your family.

☐ **BEST FRIEND:** Send this person five to seven pictures of all your worst face angles with a caption like, "You're the only person in the world I would trust to send these to. Thanks for loving me from all angles."

☐ **BEST FRIEND:** Write two haikus (lines with five syllables, seven syllables, five syllables). One poem will just be about this person. One poem will be about your friendship. Text your masterpieces to them or write them out and give them to your best friend.

☐ **CLOSE FRIEND:** Create a five-item bucket list of things that you want to do with this person and then ask them to write another five. Together, you will then have a Top Ten Friendship Bucket List to accomplish together. Hang it somewhere important and follow through.

☐ **CLOSE FRIEND:** Send a voice message to this person that lasts at least two minutes and tries to capture as many good things as possible in a short period of time.

☐ **CLOSE FRIEND:** Call their family and give them a secondhand compliment. Thank them for being great parents, siblings, or guardians and show appreciation for how they helped raise such a wonderful human being.

☐ **FRIEND:** Send them a message with a silly, famous comparison like, "You remind me of Michelle Obama because . . ." or "Have I ever told you that your essence is just like Abraham Lincoln's because . . ."

☐ **FRIEND:** Go through your old books and find one that you think this person would like. Write a little note on the inside cover about why you are passing it on.

☐ **FRIEND:** Sit down for a conversation with them (or phone call), having prepared two questions regarding two things you don't know. You can ask things like, "Who is the most important role model in your life?" or "What is your favorite weird thing about yourself?"

☐ **SOMEONE YOU ADMIRE:** Film a video of yourself talking about something you've learned from this person and how it's made you a better person. Tag this person in the video and, if possible, send them a direct message with your gratitude.

☐ **SOMEONE WHO MAKES YOU LAUGH:** Draw a picture on a small piece of paper that represents a funny memory you have with this person. Deliver it or post it online so they can see and reminisce on the moment and/or how bad of an artist you are.

☐ **A PERSON WHO INSPIRES YOU:** Try something new today based on this person's inspiration. Do it for ten minutes, take a picture or video or journal about your experience, and (if possible) share with this person about how their life has inspired you to make your life that much cooler.

☐ **A PERSON YOU DISAGREE WITH:** Send this person a text or a call that sounds something like this: "I know we differ in our perspective of _____, but I do appreciate how _____ challenges me to _____."

☐ **A ROLE MODEL YOU KNOW PERSONALLY:** Give this person a call and let them know these three things: (1) why your life has been made better because of them, (2) what you've learned from being around them, and (3) how you will continue to improve because of their incredible-ness.

☐ **A ROLE MODEL YOU'VE NEVER MET:** Go back and reread or rewatch something that this person has done or created that inspires you. Share it with one other person so they can be inspired, too!

☐ **A NEIGHBOR:** Create an IOU card that has your name, a way to contact you, and a silly offer that says you'd be willing to help with something like watching their dog, plucking some weeds, or bringing over some extra milk when they've poured cereal and realized they were out.

☐ **A PUBLIC SERVANT:** "Prank call" someone who is a public servant and just let them know that you are grateful for the work they do to keep things running—safe, fair, or whatever their job helps with.

☐ **A CAUSE:** Donate today to a cause that means something to you. If you have the ability, write an email to the person who runs it or started it and explain why you believe in their work.

☐ **TEACHER:** Create a care package for a local school that includes some tea, vitamins, and gift cards (if you can) with a note of gratitude for the work they do.

☐ **COWORKER:** Create a group text with some people who know your coworker and prompt everyone to share one good thing about this person to celebrate them just because.

☐ **STRANGER:** Leave a Kind note on a receipt or napkin for a waiter/waitress or the person serving lunch.

☐ **STRANGER:** Write a short, anonymous poem about why the world is beautiful and why everyone deserves Kindness and post it in a public space.

☐ **MYSELF:** Write down a list of your five favorite moments over the last thirty days and put it in a place to remind yourself of the power of Kindness. Make it look nice so you can stare at it often and post it proudly. Share this list with someone you care about and tell them they would be really good at this whole Thirty Days of Kindness thing.

May ideas like these spark your creativity and ignite your compassion. Thirty Days of Kindness sets a strong foundation for a Kinder lifestyle. I offer it because it's important to try a variety of Kindnesses to have some data before you begin Phase 2: The 1% Shift.

The 1% Shift

When I picture a large-scale Kindness change in our world, I see a whole lot of individuals choosing to shift their time—their priorities—by 1 percent. I envision a world where everyone puts *Kind* at the top of their To-Be List, and it holds just as much value as whatever is on their to-do list that day. This requires everyone to acknowledge that, in order to Make Kindness Normal in the world, it first requires people to Make Kindness Normal for themselves. It is an effort that doesn't happen overnight and it certainly doesn't occur in comfort or convenience.

A new normal is the by-product of the intentional stretching of ourselves to practice something small, relentlessly, until it starts to be muscle memory. It's a basketball player's layup or a card player's shuffle. And only once we have mastered this small habit should we begin to add anything more. Let the *1 percent* thrive before moving on to *2*.

Incremental improvement will always be more powerful than incidental, occasional action.

To get you inspired into taking on this ongoing practice, here are some of my favorite examples of how to begin the 1% Shift toward Kindness.

- A girl in California bakes cakes weekly for birthdays in her community.
- A girl in Louisiana does a daily gratitude video with her mom and shares it on social media.
- A man in Maine wrote a postcard to his two daughters every day. For eight years.
- A student in Washington volunteered daily to hold the door open at the local school.
- My mom wrote on a Post-it Note and included it with my lunch, daily, my whole school career (until college. Then it was a daily phone call).
- A man in California sends birthday videos, daily, to each person in his Facebook community who is celebrating.
- A teacher in Washington started checking in on how his students were doing on a scale of one to five each week, and used that data to follow up on celebratory or challenging things.
- A young man in Oregon would study the yearbook and learn one new name a day at his large school.

The habitual, targeted, ongoing exercise of a thing is what can take an idea from Confetti Kindness to Deep Kindness. Going from occasional occurrences to a deliberate practice is how we make Kindness *our* normal. It is embodiment—going from something we *do* to something we *are*—that makes it Deep.

Determined, practiced, habitual Kindness is the kind the world needs.

Conclusion

A KINDER WORLD

I'm in the Hot Dog Seat. The plane has landed and, at some point in the flight, Helga has fallen asleep. She's just waking up as people are anxiously stretching their legs and standing up under the overhead bins like Atlas himself, head crooked and hoisting the weight of a few carry-ons.

I smile at her as I hop into the aisle, already thinking about my rental car details, how far away the hotel is, and how much sleep I will get that night. I don't even get her last name; it's very rare to know when an interaction you're having with a stranger is one that you'll want to revisit over and over. And over.

I've never spoken to Helga again.

Almost certainly, it would be a better story if I had. If, years later, I was able to tell her about how her story has helped shape mine, and about all the people I've had a chance to speak with, who now also believe in *Making Kindness Normal*. Wouldn't that be a lovely ending? But I don't even know her last name. We were just airplane friends.

The average person interacts with eighty thousand individuals over the course of their life. We certainly won't remember them all, let alone see most of them again. Isn't it profound that, in each of those small moments, it is possible that what we say or do could stick in big ways? Isn't it amazing that a four-hour plane interaction laid the foundation for the next ten years of my life? Isn't it important to remind ourselves that every day, in our seemingly forgettable moments, we might do something that is unforgettable for someone else?

I've believed in Kindness for a long time. But it wasn't until I'd heard Helga's story that I was moved to understand it more deeply and explore it more obsessively. Helga's narrative is a maddeningly clear example of what I consider one of the most destructive dynamics we face as a species: our ability to proclaim we care about something without effectively doing anything about it. Our "weakness of will." Akrasia.

There is no worse practice to give lip service to than love.

We aren't collectively making a conscious choice toward hypocrisy; we've been set up to fail. We've been convinced that Kindness is a plug-and-play tool when there needs to be a much more robust user manual. We've been sold diet pills when what we actually need is a gym membership, a trainer, and a whole lot of motivation to put in the work.

We are talking about Kindness more than ever because the world is becoming more conscious of our deep need for it. But, if the primary way we've been taught Kindness looks a lot like confetti, then we will continue to treat it like the dollar-store party poppers that are momentarily exciting, but ultimately cheap. Short-lived. Cute, but usually inconsequential. Confetti almost always leaves behind a mess that someone else will have to clean up.

And what a mess we are in.

We certainly are not beyond hope—there are incredible people all around us doing wonderous things rooted in generosity, selflessness, and compassion. Many of these circumstances and stories are well beyond my understanding or experience. But I do know there are good things happening every day that go unseen and underrated. I am a desperately eternal optimist and believe deeply in the fundamental good in people.

It's just that, at scale, we've under-complicated Kindness so much that we've confused people about the ongoing work necessary to improve it. "Throw Kindness Around Like Confetti" and other platitudes are reductionistic and make us believe that all we need for a more compassionate world is the *desire* to do good. But, as Helga would remind us, the desire to help does not always equate to appropriate action. Three thousand people's desire to be Kind did nothing to alleviate Helga's suffering.

The truth is, the kind of Kindness the world needs isn't being intentionally portrayed by the media, by our leaders, or by our textbooks. We hold a belief in the idea of Kindness that isn't matched by an allocation of our resources, time, or energy.

We need a global language for Kindness. Mark Twain elegantly reminds us that "Kindness is the language which the deaf can hear and the blind can see." But the quote itself assumes that we all agree on what Kindness is in the first place.

It's hard to know what it looks like if we rarely see it authentically celebrated, acknowledged, or unpacked in thoughtful discourse. Those meaningful moments of generosity or hope—those quiet opportunities to engage in Deep Kindness—aren't always newsworthy. The five o'clock anchor isn't talking about the stranger who stopped and cried with someone like Helga. Instead, the spotlight is almost always on Confetti Kindness—the kind of Kindness that is poppy, whimsical, and one-offish. It's the stuff of headlines, not lifelines. Balloons, stuffed animals, and day-makers.

We need more world-makers and globe-changers. We need Kindness that overcomes vast differences and shakes broken systems. We need a revolution in the way we think, talk, and act in Kindness.

Most important, we must be equipped with the right vocabulary (and personal fortitude) to ask ourselves, "What gets in the way?" In order to improve at anything, we have to know what obstacles we need to overcome. I can't train for a race I don't understand.

A Kinder world is an urgent priority. We must redefine Kindness to acknowledge it as an essential quality for a functioning and flourishing world. It cannot be a nice-to-have. We have to declare it a must-have. A must-teach. A must-practice.

So, what does this road to revolution look like? How do we shape a more selfless world?

- **STEP ONE:** *Admit we have a problem.* We must first acknowledge the gap between what we believe is good and what we are actually good at if we are ever going to close it. Owning this idea personally leads to motivated action. Owning this collectively leads to the systems change necessary for long-term success.

- **STEP TWO:** *We are what we teach.* In 2016, I started CharacterStrong alongside one of my greatest mentors and best friends, John Norlin. We focus on teaching social-emotional skills and character traits in schools to help more effectively educate the Whole Person. That is to say, what skills are required outside of math, science, or reading to live our most meaningful and successful lives? If we don't make time for the explicit teaching of things like empathy, emotional regulation, or forgiveness in schools, we are leaving these foundational skills of Kindness up to crossed fingers and ill-equipped hope. Education is the number one pathway to long-term change. If we don't teach the competencies of Kindness universally, we will continue to see Kindness as the exception, not the rule.

- **STEP THREE:** *Courage is a choice, not a gift.* Most of the fears that shape our lives aren't inborn, they are invented. Culture will tell us a thousand times a day that we aren't *enough*, in order to sell us something to solve the very problem it made for us. These sorts of people-made worries predispose us to selfishness because fear, by its nature, is about self-preservation. Most of our deepest insecurities drive us away from connection instead of toward it. The normalizing of healthy sharing, vulnerability, counseling, and mental wellness is a key ingredient in accessing our most generous and Kind selves.

- **STEP FOUR:** *Purpose fuels persistence.* The research is clear: those who are resilient enough to succeed clearly know why they want to. Grit is a natural by-product of passion. Passion is the external manifestation of internal clarity of purpose. Do we take personal ownership over our definition of success, or do we let culture dictate what is most important? If we only have so much fuel to power the burners, are we willing to dedicate part of our energy—our time—to Kindness? If we don't declare Kindness as an idea worth fighting for, we will continue to exercise it only when we feel like it. And that leaves us with a world that is nice, but certainly not Kind.

- **STEP FIVE:** *1 percent change changes everything.* If a plane was en route between San Francisco and New York and flying one degree off its course, it would end up forty-three miles away from JFK airport. The difference between water becoming steam is one degree. And that one degree—that steam—can power trains and cities. Habits shape 45 percent of our life: What if we were as thoughtful about making and breaking habits that lent themselves to Kindness as we were about practicing our free throw, flossing our teeth, or getting our inbox to zero? What if the whole world committed to being 1 percent more Kind?

The kind of Kindness the world needs is available to us. It's the kind that we can teach. It's the kind that is rooted in empathy and propelled by purpose. It is the kind that is courageous in the moments where it could be complacent or complicit. It's the kind that lifts one hundred pounds in moments of need because it has lifted the tens and twenties in lots of little, quiet moments along the way.

The kind of Kindness we need is one that we've made normal in the world because we've done the hard, messy, and uncomfortable work of making it normal for ourselves.

I believe in a world where Kindness is more than confetti. A world where we value Kindness as the most important and meaningful resource we have available to us, and we treat it with the reverence, ritual, and relentless exercise that it's due. I believe in a world where the thoughtful and ongoing practice of Kindness is the number one way we measure our individual and collective successes.

I'll know we are there the next time I see someone like Helga in need, and I have to get in line to help.

Acknowledgments

This book is the by-product of many years wandering to schools and events all over the world talking about Kindness and trying to figure out how to teach it well. My first acknowledgment is to the thousands of educators who serve daily in schools and try to create more compassionate humans for a Kinder future. I'm grateful to the hundreds of thousands of students who have listened to my stories and have been a part of the sometimes clumsy process of "figuring this stuff out." I learned from all of you, and alongside you.

The team at CharacterStrong is an unreal bunch of humans. Everyone there believes in a more loving world and works relentlessly to bring that vision to life. John and Lindsay Norlin have been remarkable in their leadership and in their alignment in "living-it-out." Building this organization with them has been the culmination of decades of work, and I'm proud to serve this purpose alongside them.

I'm grateful to Chelsea Miller, who helped edit the first draft of this sprawling manuscript. She helped make my voice clearer and bolder. It then made its way to the amazing team at Tiller Press—Anja, Samantha, and Theresa have been the most selfless and supportive squad as I navigated my first publishing process. I was introduced to them by Nicole Nichols, who championed this message beyond barriers I couldn't have crossed on my own. Thanks for giving me a chance.

This whole thing is possible because of the Kindness of many. I want to acknowledge everyone who does good for others just for the sake of doing good. It's the reason you're reading this book right now and, if we do our part, I think it is that kind of unconditional Kindness today that will create a more compassionate tomorrow.

Feeling full and grateful.

—Houston

Bibliography

Borba, Michele. *Unselfie: Why Empathetic Kids Succeed in Our All-About-Me World*. New York: Touchstone, 2016.

Brown, Brené. *Rising Strong*. New York: Spiegel & Grau, 2015.

Cain, Susan. *Quiet: The Power of Introverts in a World That Can't Stop Speaking*. New York: Crown Publishers, 2012.

Frankl, Viktor Emil. *Man's Search for Meaning: An Introduction to Logotherapy*. Boston: Beacon Press, 1973.

Warner, Jennifer. "Sleep Deprivation Stirs Up Emotions." WebMD, from the WebMD archives dated October 22, 2007. Accessed January 12, 2020. https://www.webmd.com/sleep-disorders/news/20071022/sleep -deprivation-stirs-up-emotions.

Notes

CHAPTER 2: OUR PERSPECTIVES DRIVE OUR PRACTICES

1. Lera Boroditsky, "Language and the Brain," *Science* 366, no. 6461 (October 4, 2019): 13, https://science.sciencemag.org /content/366/6461/13.

CHAPTER 4: "THE EMPATHY GAP"

1. "Studies Show Normal Children Today Report More Anxiety than Child Psychiatric Patients in the 1950's," American Psychological Association (website), December 14, 2000, https://www.apa.org/news /press/releases/2000/12/anxiety.
2. "Time Flies: U.S. Adults Now Spend Nearly Half a Day Interacting with Media," Nielsen (website), July 31, 2018, https://www.nielsen .com/us/en/insights/article/2018/time-flies-us-adults-now-spend -nearly-half-a-day-interacting-with-media.
3. "The Human Brain Is Loaded Daily with 34 GB of Information," Tech 21 Century (website), December 24, 2016, https://www.tech21 century.com/the-human-brain-is-loaded-daily-with-34-gb-of -information.
4. "Studies Show a 40% Decline in Empathy Among College Students," Teaching Empathy (blog), Twenty One Toys (website), n.d., https:// twentyonetoys.com/blogs/teaching-empathy/empathy-decline-college -students.
5. Teresa Belton, "What Happens When We Shield Kids from Boredom," *Greater Good Magazine*, October 13, 2016, https://greatergood.berk eley.edu/article/item/what_happens_when_we_shield_kids_from _boredom.
6. Belton, "What Happens When We Shield Kids from Boredom."

CHAPTER 5: THE LONELY GENERATION

1. Ellie Polack, "New Cigna Study Reveals Loneliness at Epidemic Levels in America," Cigna (website), May 1, 2018, https://www.cigna.com /newsroom/news-releases/2018/new-cigna-study-reveals-loneliness -at-epidemic-levels-in-america.
2. Turhan Canli, "How Loneliness Can Make You Sick," Psychological Science Agenda newsletter, American Psychological Association (website), September 2017, https://www.apa.org/science/about/psa/2017/09 /loneliness-sick.

3. Frank John Ninivaggi, "Loneliness: A New Epidemic in the USA," *Psychology Today*, February 12, 2019, https://www.psychologytoday.com/us/blog/envy/201902/loneliness-new-epidemic-in-the-usa.

CHAPTER 6: "A CULTURE OF PERSONALITY"

1. Live Science Staff, "Personality Set for Life By 1st Grade, Study Suggests," LiveScience (website), August 6, 2010, https://www.livescience.com/8432-personality-set-life-1st-grade-study-suggests.html.

CHAPTER 7: WHAT GETS IN THE WAY?

1. Maria Popova, "Alain De Botton on Existential Maturity and What Emotional Intelligence Really Means," Brain Pickings (website), n.d., https://www.brainpickings.org/2019/11/25/the-school-of-life-book/.

CHAPTER 9: EMOTIONAL REGULATION—CHOOSING HOW WE THINK

1. Ross W. Greene, "Kids Do Well If They Can," Information Children (website), March 8, 2018, https://www.informationchildren.com/kids-do-well-if-they-can/.
2. Ross W. Greene, *Lost and & Found: Helping Behaviorally Challenging Students (and, While You're At It, All the Others)* (San Francisco, CA: Jossey-Bass, 2016).
3. Pamela M. Cole, Margaret K. Michel, and Laureen O'Donnell Teti, "The Development of Emotion Regulation and Dysregulation: A Clinical Perspective," *Society for Research in Child Development* 59, 2-3 (February 1994): 73–102, https://srcd.onlinelibrary.wiley.com/doi/abs/10.1111/j.1540-5834.1994.tb01278.x.
4. Arlin Cuncic, "How to Develop and Practice Self-Regulation," Verywell Mind (website), updated January 20, 2020, https://www.verywellmind.com/how-you-can-practice-self-regulation-4163536.

CHAPTER 10: EMPATHY—STANDING IN THE RAIN

1. Brandy Kessler, "Newtown Inundated with Teddy Bears, Stuffed Animals," *Oakland Press*, December 22, 2012, https://www.theoaklandpress.com/news/newtown-inundated-with-teddy-bears-stuffed-animals/article_e63816ee-8023-5b6c-92bb-a7426da9884d.html.

CHAPTER 12: FORGIVENESS—PEOPLE AND THEIR BEHAVIORS

1. Brené Brown, "Brené Brown: 3 Things You Can Do to Stop a Shame Spiral," *Oprah's Lifeclass*, Oprah Winfrey Network, filmed October 6, 2013, https://www.youtube.com/watch?v=TdtabNt4S7E.
2. David Foster Wallace, "'This Is Water' by David Foster Wallace (Full

Transcript and Audio)," 2005, Farnam Street (website), n.d., https:// fs.blog/2012/04/david-foster-wallace-this-is-water/.

PART 4: INSECURITY

1. Jon Simpson, "Finding Brand Success in the Digital World," *Forbes*, August 25, 2017, https://www.forbes.com/sites/forbesa gencycouncil/2017/08/25/finding-brand-success-in-the-digital -world/#7cab7ea0626e.
2. Rich Bellis, "Why It's So Hard to Pay Attention, Explained by Science," *Fast Company*, September 23, 2015, https://www.fastcompany .com/3051417/why-its-so-hard-to-pay-attention-explained-by -science.

CHAPTER 14: FAILURE—ELEVATORS, VULTURES, AND THE TERROR OF NOT DOING IT RIGHT

1. Daniel Engber, "Is 'Grit' Really the Key to Success?," Slate, May 8, 2016, http://www.slate.com/articles/health_and_science/cover _story/2016/05/angela_duckworth_says_grit_is_the_key_to_success _in_work_and_life_is_this.html.
2. Kendra Cherry, "What Psychology Says About Why Bystanders Sometimes Fail to Help," Verywell Mind (website), February 24, 2020, https://www.verywellmind.com/the-bystander-effect-2795899.
3. Kevin Carter, "Starving Child and Vulture | 100 Photographs | The Most Influential Images of All Time," *Time*, 1993, http://100photos .time.com/photos/kevin-carter-starving-child-vulture.
4. Susan Ratcliffe, in *Concise Oxford Dictionary of Quotations* (Oxford: Oxford University Press, 2011), 389.

CHAPTER 16: SHAME—THE SCARCITY OF "ENOUGH"

1. David Sedaris, "Laugh, Kookaburra: A Day in the Bush, a Night at Home," *New Yorker*, August 24, 2009, https://www.newyorker.com/ magazine/2009/08/24/laugh-kookaburra.

CHAPTER 17: BUSY—MAKING TIME FOR LUNCH NOTES

1. Laura Vanderkam, "Are You As Busy As You Think?," *Wall Street Journal*, February 22, 2012, https://www.wsj.com/articles/SB10001424052 9702033587045772376038533946544.
2. J. M. Darley and C. D. Batson, "From Jerusalem to Jericho: A Study of Situational and Dispositional Variables in Helping Behavior," Babson .edu, n.d., http://faculty.babson.edu/krollag/org_site/soc_psych/darley _samarit.html.

3. Will Durant, *The Story of Philosophy: The Lives and Opinions of the Great Philosophers of the Western World* (New York: Simon & Schuster Paperbacks, 2005).

CHAPTER 18: EXHAUSTION—OVERCONSUMPTION AND OVERWHELM

1. Yasmin Anwar, "Sleep Loss Linked to Psychiatric Disorders," UC Berkeley News, October 22, 2007, https://www.berkeley.edu/news /media/releases/2007/10/22_sleeploss.shtml.

CHAPTER 19: FIGHT VERSUS FEELINGS—PURPOSE FUELS PERSISTENCE

1. "The Whole Child Virtual Summit—Dr. Angela Duckworth," hosted by CharacterStrong, YouTube, March 30, 2020, https://www.youtube .com/watch?v=f2LUeQ0PiJs&list=PLTWAboaNpZBduSFG1WgXTI XxQ_ujfhCbW&index=4&t=4s.

PART 6: CONSISTENCY

1. Charles Duhigg, *The Power of Habit: Why We Do What We Do in Life and in Business* (New York: Random House, 2012).
2. Ibid.

CHAPTER 20: INTERSECTIONAL THINKING— BREAKING FREE FROM CHIPOTLE CHICKEN PASTA

1. Gary Chapman, *The Five Love Languages: How to Express Heartfelt Commitment to Your Mate* (Chicago: Northfield Publishing, 1995).

DEEP KINDNESS

A REVOLUTIONARY GUIDE

FOR THE WAY WE THINK, TALK,

AND ACT IN KINDNESS

HOUSTON KRAFT

Introduction

What does it mean to be kind with a capital *K*? In *Deep Kindness*, speaker, educator, and Kindness advocate Houston Kraft presents a case for a type of Kindness that is rooted in mindfulness, patience, attention, and action. In an increasingly digitally connected world, people are lonelier and more anxious than ever, and Kindness is more essential than ever. Kraft shares stories of his experiences at schools across the country, along with action plans that people can incorporate into their lives to practice the type of Kindness the world needs to heal. In *Deep Kindness*, readers learn that to be compassionate goes beyond being nice, and that the Deep Kindness the world needs is based on courage, empathy, resilience, forgiveness, and so much more.

Questions for Group Discussion

1. On pages 6 and 7, the author states: "I want to live in a world where Kindness is the baseline—a world where everyone is capable of meeting the basic human need for attention, hopefulness, and care." Discuss how you reacted to this line upon first reading it. Did it feel like a realistic desire? Does it seem attainable? Why or why not? How has your perspective changed after having read the entire book?

2. The final paragraph of page 9 poses a series of questions for readers to consider: *So what is your definition of Kindness? And perhaps the more important question: How does your definition of Kindness shape the way you interact with it in the world?* Spend time thinking about and discussing answers to these challenging questions.

3. The author claims on page 11 that "one of the biggest barriers to a Kinder world is the way we speak about Kindness." He explains on page 10 that phrases such as "Throw Kindness around like confetti" simplify the practice of Kindness, making it sound easy, and "as a result, there is a glaring delta between perceived importance and actual action." Rephrase this statement and discuss its meaning.

4. On pages 11 and 12, the hallmarks of Deep Kindness are presented. Reread this block of text and discuss one aspect of Deep Kindness that you feel is the most important, one aspect that you feel you currently practice in your life, and one aspect that you could begin to practice or improve. The author believes that Deep Kindness requires empathy and perspective-taking, resilience, courage, and forgiveness. Discuss the meaning of these requirements, and what each mean to you on a personal level.

5. In chapter 4, "The Empathy Gap," the author makes the case that the "sharp decline in our ability to show empathy pairs serendipitously with various tech inventions" such as smartphones and social media, and that while the world at large is more digitally connected, human beings are "also more isolated and anxious." Discuss the presence of technology in your life. How high does it rank in comparison to other interests you value? How much time and effort do you make to "cultivate" a "carefully crafted version" of yourself (page 19)? How might your time and effort be better used to practice Deep Kindness?

6. Discuss the fundamental differences between "a culture of character" and a "culture of personality," as discussed on page 23.

7. On page 25, the author claims that "The kind of Kindness the world needs is rooted in a desire for the common good." What does the "common good" mean to you, and how, as one person on a planet of billions, can you make a shift toward that vision? Discuss how this relates to what the author says on page 27: "The widening gap between moral knowing and Kind action is a quiet epidemic that many will diagnose in others, but few will treat in themselves."

8. On pages 28 and 29 of chapter 7, "What Gets in the Way," readers encounter a list of three main reasons why people choose to avoid

opportunities to practice Kindness: incompetence, insecurity, and inconvenience. "Discuss examples of these three barriers to Kindness that you've experienced in your own life, personally or from a distance.

9. On page 33, the author writes that "the conscious life, then, isn't so much about learning as it is remembering." How are paying attention and being mindful aspects of "remembering"?

10. In chapter 8, the author delves into the skill of Kind Communication and differentiates between fluffy compliments and those that are thoughtful and specific. Discuss a time when you received a compliment that affected you profoundly. Why do you think you remember this particular compliment? Think about the ways in which you pay people compliments. Are they fluffy or truly thoughtful? How can you begin to craft a "curated Kindness experience" for someone in your life (page 43)?

11. How can a person show love to someone without liking them? Re-read the section found on pages 48–51, *Emotional Regulation in Action*. Discuss how you can begin to practice the skills of mindfulness, cognitive reframing, and the building of an emotional vocabulary. What examples offered in this section seems most reasonable to incorporate into your life? Why? Discuss the word "supposed" in relation to expectations for yourself and others. The author writes: *Our expectations of what others are* supposed *to be is an attempt to deny that the only thing we really have any control over is ourselves.* Share an example from your life that illustrates this statement. Explain what the author means by this question: *And isn't life suddenly bigger (and much less self-centered) when you take the perspective of what is possible instead of making everything personal* (page 50)?

12. Discuss the quote by Daniel Goleman at the top of page 52. Do you agree or disagree? The author explains on pages 54–55 that "we all have three rather profound, everyday choices about how we engage with the world around us: apathy, sympathy, empathy." Discuss the meaning of each of these words and share examples of each emotion from your own life that you have experienced either personally or from a distance. What does Barbara Gruner mean on page 56 by "empathy gives Kindness its *why*"? The author describes the difference between what he calls "Shallow Empathy" and "Deep Empathy" on pages 56 and 57. How does knowing "*why* someone needs a certain type of Kindness" lead to Deep Empathy? How is paying attention and listening required to understand the *why*?

13. What is vulnerability? Think of a time when you were vulnerable. How did being vulnerable make you feel? How did you react, or not react, in your moment of vulnerability? In chapter 11, the author makes the case that caring is vulnerable. Consider the things that you say you care about? How do you *show* your care? How does/can caring for a person, animal, cause, belief make you vulnerable? What actions do you take (or can you take) to make your caring deep and meaningful? Discuss the author's statement on page 67: *The nature of caring involves exposing your neck (and your reputation) to the teeth of culture and to those people too fearful to be bigger than their insecurities.* What are "meaningful dreams" and why is "the choice to make them happen . . . vulnerable"?

14. Chapter 12 focuses on forgiveness, "Kindness's most understated partner." Discuss the meaning of the statement: *Forgiveness is about seeing the space* in *between the human and the hurt.* What do you think the author is referring to by "the space in between"? How are resentments roadblocks to forgiveness? Share a resentment that prevented you from forgiving someone. If you could go back and

change the past, would you have handled the situation differently? How and why?

15. Rejection, failure, embarrassment, and shame are insecurities the author tells us on page 83 that "are barriers to our connection with others." What do each of these words mean to you? How do you conduct your life and make decisions to avoid feeling these emotions? What negative self-talk do you engage in that fuels your insecurities? Discuss ways to rewire this "passive programming" that can "dictate our everyday choices" (page 84). What is cynicism, and how can rejection make a person cynical? How does cynicism stand in the way of Deep Kindness? Discuss the three building blocks of trust: empathy, authenticity, and consistency? Why are these three components necessary to truly trust another person?

16. How are what-ifs a failure-avoidance strategy? The author states on page 100 that "The kind of Kindness the world needs is the one that willingly accepts helplessness." Do you agree or disagree? Do you think that you are willing to accept being or feeling helpless? How are helplessness, vulnerability, and failure connected?

17. In chapter 15, the author examines how embarrassment can block our ability to practice Deep Kindness. Discuss the statement on page 103: *The majority of people* want *to help, but resent the minority who* actually do. Reread the lunchroom dance scene on pages 104–107. Try to place yourself in this lunchroom on this day. Who do you think you would be: the class president, the few kids who joined her, or the ones who joined in when it was safe to do so and when the risk of embarrassment was reduced to zero? Ask yourself the question the author asks of himself on page 105: *Where else in my life do I say I want to dance, but instead* I *stay seated?* If comfortable to do so, share your response with the group. How has embarrassment, or the risk of embarrassment, held a "grip on [your] goodness" (page 108)?

18. In a world of consumerism, 24/7 news and information, and the desire for more and more "likes," what is enough? Think about what it means to be "enough" in the world? How is feeling like you are enough a prerequisite for being a happy and Kind person? What does the author mean with this statement on page 110: *Shame is external commentary turned internal criticism*? Discuss an example of this from your own life. What lies that "once upon a time came from the outside" are now ones you have internalized?

19. What is the difference between "nice" and "Kind"? On page 119, the author describes a conversation with a student who believes that the difference between "nice" and "Kind" is that nice is *reactive*, while Kind is *proactive*. Do you agree or disagree? What is meant by *niceness can be the demeanor of the dismissive* on page 120?

20. On page 124, the author writes, *The things we give our time to are the things that we value. Our most finite and important resource is time, so where we put it is indicative of what we care about.* Discuss where you "put" your time. How do your choices about how you spend your time reflect what you care about? Toward the conclusion of chapter 17, on page 128, the author states that: *Every day we can choose to sacrifice even just a few seconds to the practice of being Kind.* How much of your day are you willing to sacrifice to practice Kindness?

21. Part 6 of *Deep Kindness* focuses on *consistency*, and how small changes of habit are necessary to make a "1 percent change toward a more compassionate life" (page 140). The author claims that the path to Deep Kindness begins with small changes, and asks, "What will be the one thing you can do relentlessly to start to build your habit of Kindness?" What small change can you make in your life that you can practice on a daily basis to be a Kinder person? Discuss the author's strategies for Intersectional Thinking. How do

you think these might help you begin to shift your thoughts toward consistent Kindness practice? Reread Thirty Acts of Kind on pages 148–152. Choose one act from the list that most resonates with you, and share why you find it meaningful. How can you shift your "priorities by 1 percent" to contribute to a "large-scale Kindness change in our world" (page 152)?

Extension Activities

MAKE TIME FOR NOTHING

On page 20 of *Deep Kindness*, we learn that "Neuroscience tells us that it is actually moments of boredom where empathy and creativity are cultivated. *Greater Good Magazine* argues that the in-between moments of silence, pause, or stillness when we get to daydream—a necessary vacuum of the clamor and clutter—are the empty canvas we create from." Have readers participate in the Embrace Your Boredom Challenge. For at least 15–30 minutes per day, they will put away their phones, turn off their screens, and do nothing. (Daydreaming is encouraged.) After these moments of stillness, readers will journal their experiences, such as thoughts, ideas, revelations, or anything else that rose to the surface. At the conclusion of the challenge, each reader will create a work of art in any medium that reflects their experience.

THE LONELY GENERATION

In chapter 5, readers learn that isolation leads to loneliness, and that loneliness is associated with depression and suicide. Research the correlations between the prevalence of social media with the increase in mental health challenges in the Gen Z population. Encourage readers to share their research in the form of an essay, a slide presentation, a work of visual art, a skit, etc.

SPECIFICITY INTO ACTION

Challenge readers to recall a person who made a positive impact or influence on their life: a person who they will never forget. Reread chapter 8, "The Vocabulary of Kindness—More Than 'Pretty Good'," and complete the activity. After the reread, readers can write a one-page reflection about the person and the specific experience that influenced their lives. Next, instruct readers to revise their reflection in the form of a personal letter. Pass out beautiful stationary on which to rewrite their letter. If possible and appropriate to do so, address and send the letters.

STAND IN THE RAIN

Reread chapter 10, "Empathy—Standing in the Rain." In this chapter, author Houston Kraft recalls an experience he had working with two friends who run Haiti Partners, an organization that believes in helping Haitians change Haiti through education. Research and begin working with local organizations that embrace the practices of Deep Kindness. Encourage readers to commit to at least a year of work with a humanitarian organization as a way to practice consistency and "Kindness in Action."

TO BE OR NOT TO BE

On page 127 the author writes, *Well, you can accomplish everything on your to-do list without ever really prioritizing the Who You Want To Be List.* After reading *Deep Kindness*, encourage readers to create a "to-do" list for their future selves, which might include going to college, becoming a teacher, or raising a family. Next, challenge them to create a Who I Want to Be List. Ask readers to compare the two lists and notice how they intersect and diverge. Encourage readers to share their lists with the others.